# MIND OVER MONEY

*The Fast Ticket
to Wealth and Independence*

by

**DAVE DAVIES**

Published by:
Success Dynamics Inc.
16 State St.
Montpelier, Vermont   05602

PRINTED IN THE UNITED STATES OF AMERICA
Second Printing, 1985
Third Printing, 1986

This publication is designed to provide the author's opinion in regard to the subject matter covered. It is sold with the understanding that the publisher or author is not engaged in rendering legal, accounting or other professional service. If legal advice or other expert assistance is required seek the services of the appropriate professional.

The author specifically disclaims any personal liability, loss, or risk incurred as a consequence of the use and application, either directly or indirectly, of any advice or information presented herein.

# Table of Contents

# Foreword

In my research for this book, I talked to millionaires, and I talked to folks who were just barely scraping by. I found that there was only one basic difference between them. No, it was not how much money they had! The most important difference between rich people and those who just get by is **mental attitude.**

Those who are wealthy have what I call a "Mind for Success". Take a wealthy person who has a Mind for Success, take away his cash, credit cards, and bank accounts and set him down in any city in the United States. Within a year, he will re-emerge a winner. Why? His mental attitude, added to his knowledge, gives him tremendous wealth, even when he is temporarily flat broke money-wise.

## Most of Us Are Taught to Be Poor

We were all brought up to believe certain things about work and wealth. We take these things for granted. Believing them keeps us poor.

FALSE ASSUMPTION #1: "Those who keep their nose to the grindstone and work the hardest will advance in their jobs and retire rich."

The plain truth is that only 1% of those working for someone else will earn a large enough salary to retire a millionaire. The vast majority will spend almost all their income, no matter how large or small, for day-to-day living expenses. Only those who earn enough to invest a sizeable amount annually have a shot at true wealth. Of these select people, most come from the ranks of the *self-employed*. Believe it or not, the average established mail-order entrepreneur earns as much or more than many top-ranking executives of Fortune 500 companies.

In the following chapters, you will learn a technique of creative relaxation that will develop your mind and get it ready for success. In fact, even if you are broke now, you will become a virtual "money machine" once you have absorbed the principles of this plan.

FALSE ASSUMPTION #2: "Security and wealth-building go hand-in-hand."

Nothing could be further from the truth. The truth is that there can be no profit without risk. The greater the potential profit, the greater the risk. If you are afraid of risk and love security, you will end up with neither wealth nor security. This is because true security is the ability to *make* money anytime it is needed and not the actual present possession of money. Money can be lost; the ability to make money stays with you forever.

Millions of Americans have put their hopes for security in the hands of the government. This is wrong. The individual is now and always will be accountable for his life. True security resides in one-self, not in a Federal Social Security System that is already technically bankrupt. If you plan to become wealthy, be willing to assume responsibility for yourself, accept the calculated risk, and eventually you will have a security that money can't buy.

FALSE ASSUMPTION #3: "Debt is to be avoided at all costs."

On the contrary — debt is a tool that is vitally necessary to build a fortune. If you have a great idea, an idea that will realistically take $100,000 to get started, but which should result in millions of dollars in income in the future, what do you do? Most of us would take ten years or longer working and sacrificing every day to save the $100,000. By that time, your idea is "old hat". The answer, of course, is to borrow the necessary funds and repay the loan from the profits.

You can avoid the dangers of borrowing as follows:

1. Borrow only for projects that result in a larger net return than the loan interest will cost and which will result in income sufficient to repay the principle.

2. Don't use borrowed funds for speculative investments. Borrowing money to purchase price-volatile commodities is unwise. Use of leverage is fine if prices are stable or rising, as in the purchase of residential housing. For more price-volatile investments, such as stocks or commodities, borrowing can be lethal.

FALSE ASSUMPTION #4: "Frugality and saving is a waste of time".

We have now come full circle. Ben Franklin said, "A penny saved is a penny earned". Today, the common practice is to spend all or more than you earn because people believe that inflation will just destroy their savings anyway. Young people feel that you might as well purchase a car you can't really afford now because you certainly won't be able to afford the higher prices in the future. This, perhaps, had a grain of truth in it when inflation was rampant several years ago. But even then, the person who put aside a portion of his income into inflation hedges, such as rare coins, was infinitely better off than the person who spent 101% of his income on consumer "goodies".

Why? Because each dollar one spends now is equivalent to $100 in forefeited wealth at the end of 20 years, assuming a net 26% annual rate of growth. It is easy to save $25 a week, especially when you realize that, if properly managed, that $25 will grow to $2,500 by the time you retire. My one piece of advice here is to put the money saved to work and not into a savings account. Put it into investments or enterprises that will yield at least a 26% annual rate of return after taxes and inflation. After all, you have worked for your money. Now let it return the favor by working for you. We will learn how to do this in later chapters.

In summary, our school system, our parents, and the public's misconception about wealth conspire to hold us back. Few, if any, colleges teach the art of money-making. Even business administration graduates are taught how to function effectively within the corporation, but not how to earn their own personal fortune. Most self-made millionaires are mavericks and loners who had the intelligence to scorn the traditional "wisdom", customs, values, and advice. In the first chapter, we will clear out of the way a few mental cobwebs about money and how it is made.

# ENTREPRENEUR'S CREDO

"I do not choose to be a common man.
It is my right to be uncommon—if I can.
I seek opportunity—not security.
I do not wish to be a kept citizen, humbled
and dulled by having the state look after me.

I want to take the calculated risk;
to dream and to build,
to fail and to succeed.

I refuse to barter incentive for a dole;
I prefer the challenges of life
to the guaranteed existence;
the thrill of fulfillment to the stale calm of Utopia.

I will not trade freedom for beneficence
nor my dignity for a handout.
I will never cower before any master
nor bend to any threat.

It is my heritage to stand erect,
proud and unafraid; to think and act for myself,
to enjoy the benefit of my creations
and to face the world boldly and say:
This, with God's help, I have done.
All this is what it means to be an Entrepreneur."

Official Credo of American Entrepreneurs Assr. ! ⅅ 1981

# CHAPTER 1
# How People Make Money

It is amazing to me how many people don't understand that you must **sell something**, eventually, in order to make money. In fact, other than unearned money from gambling, lotteries, gifts, and inheritance, selling something is the **only** way to make money. This may sound simplistic, but I receive letters every week like the one from the woman who said, "Please send me your latest book, but if it has anything to do with selling or mail-order, don't bother — just return my check".

If you think about it for a minute, how DO people make money?

1.  Discover a natural resource (gold, oil, diamonds, etc.,) and **sell** it or the rights to it.

2.  Invent a new product, patentable idea or technique and **sell** it or the rights to it. This kind of income is called a **royalty**.

3.  Earn commissions from **selling** something. The real estate brokers sells your house. The stock broker sells stock to you or for you. The import-export broker

helps you put buyer and seller from different countries together.

4. Buy a product in volume (wholesale) at a low price and **sell** it at a higher price (retail).

5. **Sell** labor or services. Plumbers, carpenters, night watchmen, scientists, teachers, etc., all **sell** their expertise, services, labor, and time.

6. Promotional profit. Buy someone else's services for an event, then **sell** the event. A promoter hires a rock and roll band, for instance, and a place for them to play. He then advertises and **sells** tickets to the concert. The owner of a football team is really an owner-promoter. He owns the team, rents the stadium, and **sells** tickets to the games.

7. **Sell** the temporary use of something you own. The landlord collects rent because he owns an apartment complex. In its purest form, the investor rents out his money to a bank for a guaranteed interest. The bank, in turn, rents out this money to a business needing working capital. The bank charges more interest than it pays the investor because it assumes a greater risk.

That's **all** there is to making money, and it all involves **selling** something.

The woman who wrote the letter quoted above also seemed put off by the concept of "mail-order". But what is mail-order? It is nothing more nor less than the ordering, either by phone or mail, and the shipping of products. Ninety-eight percent of all business involves mail-order in some form or another.

Your local grocery store orders a load of avocados from California. They are shipped by truck to the store and sold, hopefully at a profit. The store mails the produce distributor a check. All but a few of the smallest home or farm-based businesses rely on mail-order to some extent.

A person who grows fresh produce on his farm and sells it all from a roadside stand probably doesn't use mail-order to operate his business. However, he should! An example of this is Dakin Farm in Charlotte, Vermont. Initially, they sold their Vermont maple syrup, cheese, and hams only from a roadside stand. Five years ago, they grossed about $25,000 in this fashion. Today, they are the country's largest retailer of Vermont maple syrup and other Vermont-made products and have gross sales well over one million dollars a year. Ninety percent of their business is mail-order. If they had not expanded through mail-order selling, they would have remained a "Mom and Pop" roadside stand, eking out little more than bare subsistance.

So far, we have seen that selling something is the lifeblood of all business, and that mail-order, to one extent or another, is necessary to business. In Chapter Three, we will acknowledge that it truly does take money to make money, but we will also explore ways to get around this obstacle.

Finally, I would like to point out that if you live in a remote or rural area with few people, you must, with a few exceptions, use mail-order if you expect to make a lot of money. If you don't really *want* to make a lot of money, stop here — You are reading the wrong book!

I say this because capitalism and businesspeople are getting an undeservedly bad "rap" or reputation.

In every place, from our schools to the national media, business is portrayed as a dog-eat-dog world, where the most diabolical character succeeds at his opponents' expense. You have only to watch J.R. Ewing in an episode of Dallas to know what I'm talking about. Nothing could be further from the truth! Yet, like most cases of *misinformation*, this fallacy is spread because it contains a grain of truth.

Competition can be tough in the business world, and failure to compete in the marketplace results in business failures. While painful, this competition rewards achievers and penalizes inefficiency and incompetence. If only our government operated within the competitive constraints of a business! In a nutshell, it all comes down to the necessity of a **Win-Win** philosophy of doing business. No business can long survive with the attitude that it can profit at the consumers' expense.

For instance, Ford Motor Company failed to make a $7 redesign of the gasoline tank on the Ford Pinto, even though they *knew* that the existing design could be extremely hazardous in the event of a rear-end collision. The Federal suit and mandatory recall cost them $13.3 million. Incalculable additional millions of dollars were lost in *Goodwill*, that is, the public's trust and confidence in the company. No amount of advertising can buy this back.

The **Win-Win** philosophy simply means that both parties to a transaction should come out winners. In other words, good business means that everybody involved benefits. It also means that customers will continue to do business with you. This implies that there must be full disclosure. A person who sells his house for full market value knowing, but not disclosing, that a foul-smelling tannery is about to be built

4

next door has demonstrated a **Win-Lose** mentality. While he might make a short-term profit this time, it is equally likely that his future in the neighborhood would be less than harmonious.

Hindu philosophy speaks of Karma, the essence of the soul. It says that good or bad Karma results from the myriad good and bad deeds done over a lifetime. With a **Win-Win** philosophy, the business-person will have "good Karma", as well as a personal fortune. Keep in mind that money is a tool for good works and not an end in itself. When the making of a lot of money becomes so important to a person that he no longer uses honest and fair means to earn it, then both money and his earning of it are corrosive to the spirit. Unfortunately, many people feel that the great majority of rich people are less worthy and less moral than poor people.

Examine your own attitude. Do you believe that you can succeed with a **Win-Win** philosophy, i.e., one where both buyer and seller benefit? It is important that you do because your attitude toward having money and making money bears directly on your future success.

**Becoming wealthy is as much the result of a state of mind as of any particular technique.**

Short of winning a one in a million sweepstakes prize, there is virtually no chance for you to become wealthy unless you have developed a *mind for success*. It does not require education, nor does it call for personality. Although these assets are helpful, all that it *really* requires is the proper **Mental Attitude**.

I was fascinated to read recently about the fellow from New Hampshire, Jack Wells, who was seen on the evening news, sipping a beer while sitting in a beaten-up old chair alongside his mobile home. On the eight acres around him were 800 million used auto and truck tires that he had been collecting for ten years. The local authorities told him to remove or destroy the tires, "or else". Either way, it would have cost him around $150,000. When asked if he were worried about the situation, he said, "Nope. I figure that someone will come along sooner or later with a need for the tires, and I'll be a rich man." Believe it or not, a London consortium bought this man's tires, all 800 million of them for a small fortune. They plan to ship them to Africa, where tires are much in demand.

To the average person, this fellow seemed broke, uneducated, and faced with a monumental problem. To himself, he knew he was sitting on a fortune. Reality had simply caught up with this man's perception of himself.

Your mind is like a $150,000 computer. It just needs to be plugged in (motivated) and given a program (a set of plans leading to a goal). I intend to motivate you (charge up your computer) and provide you with a program that you can follow to attain your goals. If you reject my particular program for building wealth, remember that there are literally *thousands* of avenues to wealth, some of which must be particularly suited to your needs, circumstances, and personality.

Once you have studied the material, you should at least have developed a *mind for success* capable of perceiving the many wealth-building opportunities that abound all around you. When you follow my plan, you will make the "seed" capital necessary to pursue and succeed at any wealth-building opportunity that appeals to you.

# HERE'S SOMETHING TO THINK ABOUT

# CHAPTER 2
# Developing A Mind For Success

"If You Think . . . YOU CAN!

If you think you're beaten, you are,
    If you think you dare not, you don't.
If you'd like to win, but think you can't,
    It's almost for sure you won't.

If you think you're losing, you've lost.
    For out in the world we find —
Success begins with a person's will,
    It's all in the state of mind.

If you think you're outclassed, you are,
    You've got to think high to rise.
You have to stay with it,
    In order to win the prize.

Life's battles don't always go,
    To the one with the better plan,
For more often than not, you will win,
    If only you think you can."

Kristone

Once you have developed your own Mind for Success, nothing that you truly want to accomplish will be impossible for you. Failure to begin by developing your Mind for Success prior to tackling a specific money-making plan will *inevitably* result in failure. Letters from readers testify to this truth every day. One man wrote, "Yours is the 17th money-making plan I've ordered. So far none of them have worked. I sure hope yours is different!".

Relax! This plan *does work*, and it has been **proven** to work over and over again by those who have used it to develop a Mind for Success. To develop your own Mind for Success, there are four truths you must know.

1.   The **First Truth** is that you deserve to succeed and that being rich is *good*.

How often have we been told that the rich are selfish, greedy, and the oppressors of the poor? I know that the Communists in the USSR would love to have us accept this lie. How often do the newspapers pit the mean, old landlord against the poor, down-trodden tenant on welfare? The tenant had never trained to get a job, so nobody will hire him. He has always lived on other peoples' taxes (welfare). With his rent three months behind, he is finally thrown out by the "greedy" and "heartless" landlord.

Whose fault is this anyway? Certainly it is not the landlord's fault. He studied hard in school to make something of himself instead of wasting his time on the streets. He apprenticed himself to an expert and accepted less than minimum wage so that he could become expert at his trade or profession. He worked ten or more hours a day, six days a week and made other personal sacrifices so that he could buy the apartment house. He is *entitled* to a fair monetary return for his efforts, sacrifices, and monetary investment. He pays taxes on both his income and the real estate. After losing three months' income from the apartment, he finally throws the bum out. But, you guessed it! The public and the media usually side with the tenant.

If you instinctively side with the tenant and not with the landlord in the above example, you may have to work hard on Lesson 1. The truth is that you and only you are responsible for your present status, whether you be the unemployed bum out on the streets or the rich landlord.

>TOUGH LESSON #1: If you succeed, you deserve the credit. If you are presently broke and a failure, don't lay the blame on those who are succeeding, but try to succeed yourself. Ultimately, you, and you alone are responsible for yourself and your status in life.

>TOUGH LESSON #2: Self-sacrifice is not necessarily good.

Under the **Win-Win** philosophy, it is wrong to sacrifice your own interests for another's. Doing so results in a **Lose-Win** situation. A businessperson who sacrifices his profit so that his customers get a better deal will soon find himself out of business, unemployed, and a burden on society. We are told that to put yourself first is selfish. But who, honestly, is more important to yourself than you?

The problem is that people fail to realize that you can put your own interests first and still be a warm, loving, sharing, and completely honest human being. Believe me, you are number **One.** Your family is more important that any other family in the world. It is both your moral right and your obligation to yourself and your family to succeed! As long as your success is a **Win-Win** success, everybody benefits. So why not succeed? Success and life itself are synonymous. To live is to grow spiritually, mentally, and financially. To grow rich in *all* these areas is the true meaning of both life and success.

2. The **Second Truth** is that you *have the power* to do whatever you set your mind to doing.

A modern computer would have to be 10,000 times larger than your brain to equal its capacity. Unfortunately, on the average, most of us use just 2% of our full mental resources. Learn to tap the unused 98% of your brain's capacity.

The other day, the TV show "That's Incredible" showed a man who had memorized the entire Los Angeles telephone directory, which contained several million names. Not only that, you could give him any name, and he would immediately tell you that person's telephone number and street address. He could also tell you what page you were looking at and all the adjacent names on the page.

I personally knew a young woman in San Diego with prodigious mathematical powers. She had dropped out of high school, yet she could take any series of numbers, add them together, and then multiply them by each other in her head with total accuracy. I tested her and found that she was faster than a mathematician with a calculator! All of us have the mental capacity — more than we will ever need for any task!

3. The **Third Truth** is that you must cultivate a *burning desire* to be successful, in your own terms.

By desire, I am not talking about wishing for success or dreaming of better luck. I am talking about single-minded commitment to a goal. This kind of commitment means that you sacrifice *whatever it takes* (other than your basic values) in order to achieve your goals.

Ironically, once you firmly set a course on the road to success, your mind is happy. Your mind needs focus and purpose in order to operate at peak capacity. As you achieve, step by step, the goals you set out to reach, each additional step becomes easier and more and more automatic. Success can actually become a habit, but, like all habits, it requires consistent and motivated practice. It always puzzled me that my father would routinely bring along his briefcase when we were on vacation. He would work, sometimes for hours a day, while all around him, people were swimming and otherwise relaxing. Recently, I understood when he admitted that, for him, working *was* relaxing. Once you have a *burning desire* to achieve your goal, you will find that it is more satisfying to work 12 hours a day towards your personal goal than to work 8 hours a day at a job helping somebody else reach his own goal, and just barely scraping by financially to boot!

4.  The **Fourth Truth** is that once you are motivated to act, you **Must Act!**

Simple, isn't it? Yet most of us seem to excel in one thing — procrastination! This is where computers have us beaten. When instructed to run a program, a computer proceeds to accept input data, analyse the data, and provide the output or answers demanded of it almost instantly.

Too often, our good intentions get bogged down when it comes time to put dreams into practice. The solution is to break your goals down into daily tasks. Each morning, make a list of the tasks to be done, arranging the list according to priority. Million dollar goals are attained step by step, one step at a time, one simple task after another. Build the habit of immediately doing the tasks you have assigned yourself. Use the mental prod: **Do It Now**. Any time you begin to hesitate, say to yourself, **"Do It Now"**, and proceed immediately to **Do It**.

By routinely using this technique, it will soon become a strong habit. Once you have told yourself, **"Do It Now"**, *never* fail to follow it up with action. This technique is called "reinforcement" by psychologists. The mind accepts the sequence of mental prod followed by action until it actually becomes difficult *not to act* after repeating **Do It Now**! Just as years of repetition of difficult and complicated moves and countermoves in Karate will eventually enable the practitioner to advance to the high rank of Black Belt, the constant practice of proper money-making attitudes eventually makes successful money-making a habit, just the same as any other good habit.

To summarize this chapter so far, the following four basic truths will be the foundation of your success:

1. Success is *good*. It is synonymous with life itself. You deserve to live and live well!
2. You have the power to do whatever you decide to do.
3. You must set *specific goals* for yourself and cultivate an *overwhelming desire* to accomplish them.
4. You must *Act* by following a specific plan to achieve your goals.

# CHAPTER 3
# Creative Mental Imaging

Seven years ago, I learned something that changed my life. I learned that not only was I responsible for my actions, but that I could *choose* my thoughts and attitudes. By choosing what I thought, I was enabled to channel my actions toward success.

What excites you? Do you dream of being outgoing and popular or wealthy and respected? If something excites you, you can dream about it. If you can dare to dream of the perfect you and imagine yourself living that dream, you *can* fulfill your dream in reality.

The key to this process is, first, to let yourself go. Just relax and picture your ideal life. A relaxation technique that works for me is to turn on a fan or air conditioner that runs with a background hum. This "white noise" helps block out extraneous sounds. There are also records and tapes of waves rolling in from the ocean that can be very soothing. I do not recommend background music, as most of today's music is exciting and distracting, rather than calming.

Find a comfortable chair (a recliner is good.) in a private place in your house. Lie back and take five or six deep breaths. Concentrate on your toes. Picture the blood flowing through them. You should feel them tingle. Tighten up your toes and legs. Flex all the muscles as hard as you can for about 8 seconds. Relax your muscles suddenly and completely. Trace the feeling of relaxation up from your toes, through your ankles, to your calves, your knees, thighs, and buttocks. Tighten your buttocks and stomach muscles. Tighten your chest, shoulders, arms, and fists. Now, suddenly relax completely.

Close your eyes, breathe deeply, and hold your breath for a count of four. Breathe again, even more deeply, and hold it for a count of six. Breathe very deeply. Hold your breath for a count of eight, then exhale and relax completely. Next, allow your mind to float. Picture your ideal life. Be realistic. Picture yourself doing the things you would love to do, day after day. Living on the beach in Tahiti may sound great in commercials, but do you *really* want to live in a grass hut on the other side of the planet? Close your eyes and picture every detail of your ideal life.

Perhaps you have always wanted to paint pictures. Imagine your ideal studio overlooking the ocean. See the canvasses, the skylight; feel the polished wood of the floor of your studio; listen to the sounds of the ocean below your window. Then experience the thrill of going to your own first art exhibit, hearing the praise of the critics and, perhaps, even selling a few paintings. We used to call this daydreaming. Today, I call it **Creative Mental Imaging** (CMI). By the time we reach the age of 7, our ability to daydream has been stunted by misguided parents and school systems. The truth is:

> **All creative thought involves imagining what is now and then what could and should be.**

Inventions, art, music, scientific theories, and better ways of doing everyday things begin in the mind, in the *imagination*, of their creator. Creativity depends on imagination. Is creativity necessary for financial success? No. You can make money by imitating or by employing successful creators. You must, nevertheless, learn to program your own mind by picturing your success and then backtracking through the steps necessary to bring it about.

## Become the Best You Can Be

Did you know that if you were to imagine throwing a perfect basket from the foul line fifty times in succession, you could then actually take a basketball and throw it *more* accurately than if you had actually practiced throwing it fifty times? In the same way, were you to visualize every day a suave, more confident, more successful you, that new self would gradually emerge and become reality. Cary Grant has been under-rated as an actor. He always seemed to be playing himself — a suave, capable gentleman. But Cary Grant wasn't born into a sophisticated upper class family. He escaped from an impoverished home life by joining an acrobatic troupe. Eventually, he *created* the persona, or image, that led to his popularity in the movies. It wasn't until later that he actually became the poised, confident man he portrayed on the screen. One might, indeed, say that he is a self-made man!

Be yourself, but be the best that you can be. And that best is literally anything you yourself can visualize and to which you can aspire!

You already know that your mind is like a computer. Like a computer, your mind accepts and stores certain data — data which collectively helps you in forming your own opinion of yourself, your self-image. If, from Year One of infancy, everyone around you kept telling you that you are no good, stupid, and that you won't amount to much, chances are that this is what you will believe. And, chances are that this is how you will behave.

Unfortunately, life has a way of dealing out self-fulfilling prophesies. The infant becomes a trouble-making brat. Neighbors and teachers run the child down. By adolescence, he has proven them right; he drops out of high school to bum around. We are all bombarded daily with garbage from people who perceive us in a certain way and then treat us accordingly. A man with a hearing problem is treated as though he is a moron. A young woman doctor is told, "Nurse, I want a second opinion, preferably from a man."

## Steps to Prepare Your Mind for Success

1. Take stock of who you are. Coldly, analytically, look at your personal strengths and weaknesses.

2. Use CMI to picture the person you wish to be. Live the life you long for and actually feel every detail of it in your imagination.

3. Practice acting *as if you had already become your ideal self.* NOTE: This is easier with strangers and acquaintances. Close friends and family may resist your efforts to change.

4. Become aware of those close to you who "bring you down". Don't accept their input automatically if it is derisive or demeaning. When necessary, correct them and/or yourself. If there is a grain

of truth in their attitude (They called you a clutz when you spilled your coffee for the third time in a week), examine your actions. If your actions don't agree with your ideal self, visualize an improved self.

Were you to visualize yourself as a person worthy of respect, you will soon command the respect of others. Friends who never took you seriously will either recognize your new status or cease being worthy to be your friends. You don't need friends who lack respect for you. Surround yourself with people whom you respect and who respect you.

## Be Positive. You Have Everything to Gain

Much has been written about Positive Mental Attitude (PMA), yet it is not taught in our schools. Few parents know of or practice the principle. This is unfortunate. It is a basic truth that something cannot and will not be done by one who thinks it to be impossible. This is another example of the self-fulfilling prophecy. When was the last time you brought your car to a garage for repair and had the mechanic give you three reasons why he couldn't repair it? Naturally, your car didn't get fixed — not at that establishment at any rate.

When someone begins by listing all the problems he might encounter or reasons why he can't do a job, I move on *immediately*. I don't waste time on **Can't Doers**. You shouldn't either. And that includes yourself. Take stock. Are you a **Can't Doer**? Virtually everything you are likely to attempt *can be done*, one way or another. Problems are simply solutions waiting to be discovered.

Ultimately, you must think positively because

thinking negatively is NOT PROFITABLE! All activity has obstacles. Accept boulders in your path for what they really are, the stepping-stones to success. You won't climb the ladder of success by complaining that the rungs are too far apart. You *will* get to the top either by adding extra rungs or by building a ramp.

*Remember the Cosmic Truth:*

**Every adversity carries with it the seed of an equivalent or greater benefit.**

There is no such thing as failure, only temporary setbacks, all of which carry the seed of a greater benefit. For the person with a Mind for Success, each setback is not a stumbling block, but a *building block* upon which his future success is built.

> EXERCISE:   Every day, practice eradicating the word "can't" from your vocabulary. If you turn down a challenge, it must be because you don't desire to do it, rather than because you cannot do it.

## Choose Success

Successful living is a matter of choice. Conscious choices are made every step of the way. There are no easy answers, but, from my vantage point, it appears to be tougher to live the life of a failure than to work your way up to success (I've tried both, so I should know). Remember, once you have developed the success habit, maintaining it is pretty much creative imagination and repetition. The steps to success can be repeated over and over again, with but slight variations, in order to continue the wealth-building process. Once you have personally developed a concept, it is entirely possible to have others implement your plans for you while you relax and grow rich.

We have seen how it is necessary for you to let

yourself go on an imaginary creative spree, creating for yourself the best that life has to offer. Now it is time to fill in the blanks.

Were you to set out in your car on a trip, the very first question to answer is, "What is my destination?". You now know your destination. CMI has provided that for you. Now you must plan your route and prepare both your means of transport and yourself for the journey.

Most people spend less time planning their future than planning a vacation. Some people make no plans at all, but follow the path of least resistance in life. They "go with the flow". Life is full of opportunities, but they must be perceived and grabbed. The lucky person who has an opportunity drop into his lap is extremely rare; maybe one in a million is so lucky. Even so, if he hasn't yet developed a Mind for Success, his lucky opportunity is often wasted.

A family in San Diego was living an impoverished existence, until they were awarded $800,000 in a lawsuit. By the end of the following year, they were again dependent on welfare!

On the other hand, James Price made $300,000 on Wall Street by the time he was twenty. Like many others, he lost it all, plus $80,000 in borrowed money, in the stock market crash of 1929. But by 1932, he was worth close to a million dollars, having paid off all his debts along the way. Jim Price had PMA. To do what Jim Price did you not only need PMA — you must have clear cut goals.

## Goal Setting

When you are starting out be sure to keep your goals and ambitions to yourself. Small people just love to shoot down others' ambitions plans. Write your goals down and refer to them often. Look back at what you wrote in a month, then in a few months. Work on them constantly, and don't be afraid to revise and rewrite. Goals evolve, they don't have to be set in concrete.

Think in possibilities. What is possible for you to achieve in the next six months? And go for it! Don't play it safe with what you'll probably achieve anyway. Push yourself to go further. The rewards are greater.

Feel the winning feeling. You are successful. Wear the clothes of total accomplishment and peace of mind. Live each day as though you have already reached your goal. As you succeed replace old goals with new, more ambitious goals.

Remember, don't announce your goals. This will set you up for failure. Even if you make a pact with yourself to attain a specific goal, don't chastise yourself if you don't make it. It may have been unrealistic or you may not have put in the necessary effort.

Do it yourself. There is nobody better to help you achieve your desires than you. Tap into the power of the subconscious and practice being your own fantasy.

Write a GOAL CONTRACT for yourself. Write it to be specific and detailed. It must include realistic dated deadlines for attaining each goal. Instead of saying I will become slimmer and more physically fit say:

"I am losing and continue to lose four or more pounds each and every week, I am becoming slimmer and fitter each day by running no less than one mile each morning."

Put your statements in the *present tense* rather than the future tense. The unconscious mind takes *no action* on statements like I'm going to become rich. To make your mind perform it must be told specifically *what is desired and that action is to begin immediately* not sometime in the future.

On the next page is the specific ending to your goal contract, no matter what it may be. You should write down all the specific elements of YOUR contract and memorize them along with this ending. Repeat your entire contract three times a day, just before arising, at a quiet period during the day and just after retiring to bed. Relax and take time to visualize your goals, how you can attain them and the fruits of success. Savor your accomplishments and imagine having attained your goals.

When you have finally set your goals, your mind *automatically* begins taking steps to achieve them. By a combination of creative imagination and down-to-earth planning, the means by which to accomplish these goals will become clear.

## Dreamers versus Planners

Some of you may be saying, "That's great, Dave, but I've always been a dreamer, and I never get anything done." The solution is to analyze your goal, translate it into digestible steps, each one of which you can easily grasp, and then tackle those steps systematically, one by one. If you have difficulty keeping both feet on the ground, consult a down-to-earth professional who will sit down with you and bring your "pie in the sky" down to cold, hard facts and figures. The right professional can help you write up a business plan, which is a logical first step. But, I'm getting ahead of myself — we were discussing the result of choosing a specific, tangible goal.

You will find yourself becoming enthusiastic and

# GOAL CONTRACT

Date _____

By _____ I will have
earned a minimum of
$_____


I will have earned this amount as a result of giving the most
efficient services of which I am capable, rendering the fullest
possible quantity and the best possible quality of service in the
capacity of _____

_____


This is an irrevocable contract I make with myself.


Signed _____

possessing energy you never had before. Startling insights and new ideas will enter your mind spontaneously. While you sleep, you may even dream of solutions to difficult problems.

The following story is true: In the late 1960's, a lady mathematician in England began having dreams every night that she was in a class where the most advanced theories of genetics were being taught and made crystal clear. These dream episodes were so vivid and clear that she recorded what she had learned each night. Eventually, she sought out one of the foremost specialists in genetics. She visited him in California and, with some embarrassment, revealed her nocturnal experiences to him. He was shocked to find that her information matched his own most recent discoveries, especially since she was not trained in biology. On comparing notes, they discovered that they had been having virtually identical dreams. Both were seated in a celestial classroom, learning the secrets of DNA from the same professor. The information they shared was so advanced that it had never before been published!

The author, Taylor Caldwell, revealed that her famous true-to-life novels, such as *Dear and Glorious Physician,* were written in fits of inspiration. Some passages came to her in snatches of dreams before she was a teenager. Others were dictated to her by a mysterious inner voice. At the age of thirteen, she wrote of the legendary continent of Atlantis. In the year 1913, she described nuclear fission (even before Hahn, Mitner, and Einstein knew of it) and the hydrogen bomb. With no background in physics and just the rudiments of math, she accurately described the nature of the atom.

Never underestimate your power to achieve, once

you have set yourself a clearcut goal and have followed it up with action. You will discover that your mind has awesome powers — powers far beyond your imagination.

## How to Avoid Personal and Financial Failure

A Negative Mental Attitude (NMA) is the rejection of possibilities, the rejection of faith, and, ultimately, the rejection of life itself. Surprisingly, the person with PMA is not an optimist, but a realist. He realizes that no one is responsible for his success or failure but himself. He knows that his attitude is more important to success than *any* obstacle, whether it be lack of education, a physical handicap, or a misdirected upbringing. The person with NMA is not a realist at all.

Nearly every one of the convicts I used to counsel believe deep down that they've gotten a raw deal from the world. They believe that the world owes them a living. Almost anything they do they feel is justifiable as retribution for the real or imagined wrongs that they have suffered. The ne'er-do-well blames everyone and everything for his miserable life. He isn't a realist, for he hasn't accepted responsibility for himself. If he did just one positive thing to improve his condition each day, he would soon lose the habit of complaining because he would have so little to complain about.

When you catch yourself complaining, **stop**, and ask yourself why you are complaining. If you can change matters, change them. If you can't change matters, there's no point in complaining. Accept the situation as a *"given"* and work around it. It's as simple as that!

As a young boy, Leroy Jackson, lost his right arm

in an accident. He had watched neighborhood children playing basketball and decided that he too would like to play. Playing with just his left hand, he made the high school team. It took years of dedicated practice. His success in high school confirmed his resolve to play professional basketball, despite being one-armed and under 6′ tall. His overcompensation for his handicap resulted in his perfecting moves that few, if any, two-handed players could duplicate. And yes, he did succeed in being chosen on the basis of his playing skills alone to play professional basketball with the Harlem Globe Trotters exhibition team.

So, if you are faced with a handicap, whether it be real or imagined, physical or mental, educational or social, **fine**, simply accept it as a *given*, work around it, and you will find that what used to be a handicap can become an asset. It is up to you to make the best of it using PMA. Stop right now making excuses for your shortcomings. They are shortcomings only if you cease either to change them or compensate for them. The young basketball player knew that he could *never* use the excuse that he had only one arm if he fumbled the ball. Why? Because all that would get him was sympathy, not success. Through determination, grit, and the refusal to compromise his performance with excuses, he became an outstanding player. The person who thinks he is dumb is much more handicapped than a person with a below average IQ. The person who thinks he is unattractive is far more handicapped than the person with an actual blemish who feels self-confident. The person who believes he is a failure is far more handicapped than he who makes mistakes and learns from them.

## Commitment and Risk

It is a universal truth that the only sure things in

life are death and taxes. While civilized man has progressed somewhat from the jungle ethic, *survival of the fittest*, life is still competitive. Competition implies risk. Each step forward involves risk. The child learning to walk stumbles and falls at first. The skier may tumble and break a leg. The novice pilot may crash-land, but how can a child walk, a skier ski, or a pilot fly without risking the attempt?

**Almost no worthwhile activity is totally devoid of risk. Without risk, there can be no reward.**

People so fear the unknown risks inherent in new activities that they stagnate and head for failure through default. One such person wrote, "I am returning your book . . . as I have no interest in becoming involved in something I know nothing about." Others, myself among them, started with far less than the information in that book . . . and succeeded very well.

Courage is required to face possible failure and the unknown. Without it, Columbus would not have discovered America, and man would not have walked on the moon.

In order to succeed, you *must* be willing to risk failure. In other words, gaining success calls for 100% commitment to your goals. Therefore, choose your goals carefully, for once you are committed to achievement, you have no choice but to succeed.

In the next chapter, we will examine the adage "It takes money to make money". Is this just an excuse for "have nots", or, as in so much folk wisdom, is there a grain of truth behind it?

# CHAPTER 4
# It Takes Money to Make Money — Fact or Fiction?

I've got news for you. The much touted scheme of turning ordinary rocks into gold does not work. Several years ago, the Russians made the headlines when the news leaked out that they had succeeded in transforming ordinary lead into gold. The market price of gold plummeted $50 an ounce overnight. Then sanity returned to the market when people found out that it had cost the Russians $10 million to create .1 gram of gold, which was then worth about 80 CENTS! You can't get something for nothing, so stop wasting your time looking for the perpetual motion machine or the "get rich quick" schemes that require no investment.

"Seed money" is the closest thing to no investment that is realistically possible. This concept, **seed money,** is a universal principle. It states that a small amount of money, the seed money, must be planted (invested) in a fertile idea and nurtured carefully until it bears fruit. From the tiny acorn the mighty oak tree grows. Likewise, a tiny amount of money invested in an idea whose time is ripe can multiply so many times that the resulting profits are to the seed money as the giant oak tree is to the acorn. Occasionally, the seed money can take the form of an investment of your time, talents, ideas, and energy, but this is the exception.

Some businesses require a huge initial capital investment just to get off the ground. These include the capital-intensive heavy industries, such as steelmaking, mining, the oil industry, automobile manufacturing, airlines, etc. Most businesses require a medium investment of from $50,000 to $5,000,000. These would include restaurants, retail shops, home building, small banks, and very small insurance companies. Just a few are "bootstrap" businesses requiring little seed money, and, of those, only a handful have the potential of taking $1,000 or less in seed money and eventually turning it into a million dollar a year business.

I will state categorically that:

**your chances of succeeding in your own business rise exponentially with the quantity of seed money you control at the inception of your venture, all other things being equal.**

Under-capitalization is the largest single cause of new business failures. Seventy-six percent of new business start-ups fail within five years, according to the U.S. Bureau of Labor Statistics. In the most risky business of all, commodity trading, most professional traders refuse to trade with less than a $10,000 initial balance. So, if you are serious about getting rich, take it one step at a time. Raise at least $5,000 seed capital BEFORE going into business. Becoming wealthy is a process, not an event. Other than sweepstakes or lottery winners or those who inherit a fortune suddenly, the roster of those who become wealthy overnight can be counted on one hand.

While it *is* true that it takes money to make money, ideas are far more valuable and important. Money without ideas collects 5% interest in a passbook savings account or, perhaps, a few percent more from a money market fund. Five thousand dollars and a great idea can make you a millionaire!

To raise your initial $5,000 seed capital, there are several choices:

1. Save a portion of your current income by cutting expenses and keeping to a strict budget.
2. Convert assets to cash.
3. Moonlight with a second part-time job or business and save all the income.
4. Borrow money.
5. Any combination of the above.

The first choice is often the most difficult to implement. Those who don't believe they can ever gain great wealth, tend to choose instant gratification over long-range goals. All their available income and, often, much of their future income, is spent on current needs and desires. Yet, were you to save and invest just $1.00 a year, in just 17 years you would have a $100 nest egg @ 20% annual rate of return. Eighty-eight dollars of the hundred is the amount earned through compounding profits! Thus, every dollar spent now actually costs you $88 in lost wealth — never to be recouped. Looked at in this light, it makes extremely good sense to spend frugally and to save 10% of your income, regardless of your circumstances. See Chart No. 1.

Only when you can earn more than bank interest should you spend your savings — by investing in your own business. My motto is to spend freely *only* on things that will appreciate at a rate equal to or

| YRS | 17.0% ANNUAL RATE | 18.0% ANNUAL RATE | 19.0% ANNUAL RATE | 20.0% ANNUAL RATE | YRS |
|---|---|---|---|---|---|
| 1 | 1.000 000 | 1.000 000 | 1.000 000 | 1.000 000 | 1 |
| 2 | 2.170 000 | 2.180 000 | 2.190 000 | 2.200 000 | 2 |
| 3 | 3.538 900 | 3.572 400 | 3.606 100 | 3.640 000 | 3 |
| 4 | 5.140 513 | 5.215 432 | 5.291 259 | 5.368 000 | 4 |
| 5 | 7.014 400 | 7.154 210 | 7.296 598 | 7.441 600 | 5 |
| 6 | 9.206 848 | 9.441 968 | 9.682 952 | 9.929 920 | 6 |
| 7 | 11.772 012 | 12.141 522 | 12.522 713 | 12.915 904 | 7 |
| 8 | 14.773 255 | 15.326 996 | 15.902 028 | 16.499 085 | 8 |
| 9 | 18.284 708 | 19.085 855 | 19.923 413 | 20.798 902 | 9 |
| 10 | 22.393 108 | 23.521 309 | 24.708 862 | 25.958 682 | 10 |
| 11 | 27.199 937 | 28.755 144 | 30.403 546 | 32.150 419 | 11 |
| 12 | 32.823 926 | 34.931 070 | 37.180 220 | 39.580 502 | 12 |
| 13 | 39.403 993 | 42.218 663 | 45.244 461 | 48.496 603 | 13 |
| 14 | 47.102 672 | 50.818 022 | 54.840 909 | 59.195 923 | 14 |
| 15 | 56.110 126 | 60.965 266 | 66.260 682 | 72.035 108 | 15 |
| 16 | 66.648 848 | 72.939 014 | 79.850 211 | 87.442 129 | 16 |
| 17 | 78.979 152 | 87.068 036 | 96.021 751 | 105.930 555 | 17 |
| 18 | 93.405 608 | 103.740 283 | 115.265 884 | 128.116 666 | 18 |
| 19 | 110.284 561 | 123.413 534 | 138.166 402 | 154.740 000 | 19 |
| 20 | 130.032 936 | 146.627 970 | 165.418 018 | 186.688 000 | 20 |
| 21 | 153.138 535 | 174.021 005 | 197.847 442 | 225.025 600 | 21 |
| 22 | 180.172 086 | 206.344 785 | 236.438 456 | 271.030 719 | 22 |
| 23 | 211.801 341 | 244.486 847 | 282.361 762 | 326.236 863 | 23 |
| 24 | 248.807 569 | 289.494 479 | 337.010 497 | 392.484 236 | 24 |
| 25 | 292.104 856 | 342.603 486 | 402.042 491 | 471.981 083 | 25 |
| 26 | 342.762 681 | 405.272 113 | 479.430 565 | 567.377 300 | 26 |
| 27 | 402.032 337 | 479.221 093 | 571.522 372 | 681.852 760 | 27 |
| 28 | 471.377 835 | 566.480 890 | 681.111 623 | 819.223 312 | 28 |
| 29 | 552.512 066 | 669.447 450 | 811.522 831 | 984.067 974 | 29 |
| 30 | 647.439 118 | 790.947 991 | 966.712 169 | 1181.881 569 | 30 |
| 31 | 758.503 788 | 934.318 630 | 1151.387 481 | 1419.257 883 | 31 |
| 32 | 888.449 408 | 1103.495 983 | 1371.151 103 | 1704.109 459 | 32 |
| 33 | 1040.485 808 | 1303.125 260 | 1632.669 812 | 2045.931 351 | 33 |
| 34 | 1218.368 395 | 1538.687 807 | 1943.877 077 | 2456.117 621 | 34 |
| 35 | 1426.491 022 | 1816.651 612 | 2314.213 721 | 2948.341 146 | 35 |
| 36 | 1669.994 496 | 2144.648 902 | 2754.914 328 | 3539.009 375 | 36 |
| 37 | 1954.893 560 | 2531.685 705 | 3279.348 051 | 4247.811 250 | 37 |
| 38 | 2288.225 465 | 2988.389 132 | 3903.424 180 | 5098.373 500 | 38 |
| 39 | 2678.223 794 | 3527.299 175 | 4646.074 775 | 6119.048 200 | 39 |
| 40 | 3134.521 839 | 4163.213 027 | 5529.828 982 | 7343.857 840 | 40 |
| 41 | 3668.390 552 | 4913.591 372 | 6581.496 488 | 8813.629 408 | 41 |
| 42 | 4293.016 946 | 5799.037 819 | 7832.980 821 | 10577.355 289 | 42 |
| 43 | 5023.829 827 | 6843.864 626 | 9322.247 177 | 12693.826 347 | 43 |
| 44 | 5878.880 897 | 8076.760 259 | 11094.474 141 | 15233.591 617 | 44 |
| 45 | 6879.290 650 | 9531.577 105 | 13203.424 228 | 18281.309 940 | 45 |
| 46 | 8049.770 061 | 11248.260 984 | 15713.074 831 | 21938.571 928 | 46 |
| 47 | 9419.230 971 | 13273.947 961 | 18699.559 049 | 26327.286 314 | 47 |
| 48 | 11021.500 236 | 15664.258 594 | 22253.475 268 | 31593.743 576 | 48 |
| 49 | 12896.155 276 | 18484.825 141 | 26482.635 569 | 37913.492 292 | 49 |
| 50 | 15089.501 673 | 21813.093 666 | 31515.336 327 | 45497.190 750 | 50 |

*Chart #1 — Future Value of $1.00 Invested Each Year — Compounded Annually*

greater than current interest rates. Apply this principle to *everything* you buy. It will make you money! For example, I purchase automobiles at or below wholesale. I use them, and when I eventually sell them, I usually turn a profit-selling at full retail. My home appreciates 5% a year. It was purchased with little money down, using the principle of leverage. In the case of disposable goods, always buy quality. You get better performance and longer use. The rich follow this principle religiously. It can even be applied to furniture. Buy top quality antiques that will appreciate in value.

Apply it to cars. Invest in a restored classic or buy a used car at wholesale. An auto dealer's license can be purchased for less than $100 in many states. This gives you access to dealers' auctions and auto salvage yards where cars can be purchased below wholesale. You can purchase a slightly damaged wreck or theft recovery vehicle and have it repaired to be like new for far less than the retail cost of a similar vehicle. If you must drive a new car, stick with top quality. New Mercedes Benz and BMW automobiles depreciate less than almost all other makes.

Apply it to your housing. Never rent if you can buy. Always purchase with a minimum down payment, no more than 10%, or put more down and discount the purchase price at least 20%.

Apply it to your diet. You should eat only top-quality fresh foods. They taste better. They will keep you in better health and give you longer life and more energy.

Apply it to education. Prepare your children for a lifetime of success by accepting only the finest educational standards.

## Convert Assets to Cash

The second money-raising alternative is to convert assets to cash. Garage sales are becoming a way of life for many Americans, with good reason. We are voracious consumers of gadgets, tools, toys, and merchandise of all kinds. You yourself can probably turn up a whole garageful of merchandise you could bear to part with. Selling unwanted articles can be a relatively painless way to help raise seed capital. Holding an ongoing garage sale can actually be part of solution #3 — moonlighting with a part-time business or job. We will cover that approach in the next section.

A one-time only sale will probably not raise enough cash. If it doesn't, consider selling more valuable items through classified ads. Any item that sells for fifty dollars or more is worth listing in an ad. Items you may have stored are worth cleaning up and selling. The diamond engagement ring left you by your aunt could bring in a thousand dollars. The pickup truck you bought six years ago could bring in two or three thousand.

There are several basic rules to follow to maximize the return possible from selling possessions.

1. If you don't have a clear idea of the value of an item, have it appraised before selling it.
2. Ask slightly more than you expect to accept. If you are selling to a dealer, get three offers before selling.
3. Display an item in the best possible way. Make those simple repairs, apply a fresh coat of paint, and be sure that things are as clean and shiny as possible. Ninety percent of the public would rather buy a rusty jalopy with a fresh paint job than a solid, rust-free car with the original faded paint. Jewelers, especially, take this recommendation. They display their jewelry under indoor spotlights, usually on a

black velvet background. Even dull diamonds sparkle fabulously in this light.

4. Place ads that sell in media that sell. This is a simple recommendation, often ignored. You don't sell a 3 carat flawless diamond ring in the local shopper's weekly. Advertise in media that are read by your prospects.

Which of the following is the better ad?

A. "Selling grinder. $50, rowboat $150, bicycle, 123-1111."

B. "For sale: Black and Decker 3/4 HP prof. quality grinder. Hardly used. Sold new for $175; first $75 cash takes it. Call 123-1111."

The second ad has a clear selling description, shows what a bargain the merchandise is, and urges immediate action.

It is usually better to devote one ad to each article selling for over fifty dollars. Many people looking for a bicycle would overlook the one offered in ad A above. Always state the asking price in your ad.

## Moonlight for Second Income

The third money-raising alternative is to moonlight at a second part-time job or business and save all the income. Once you have decided that all extra income is **untouchable**, it is amazing how fast it adds up. Just $500 per month savings will provide you with $5,000 seed capital in 10 months. If you are married, your spouse could find a job and provide the new source for savings. Finding a second job shouldn't be very complicated. Don't shoot for the moon. At this point, **any** job will do. Some examples of jobs for which you can try are:

> waiter, waitress
> gas station attendant
> night watchman, store security
> sales clerk, grocery clerk
> secretary, typing service
> delivery person, delivery service
> lifeguard
> babysitter
> building maintenance
> part-time teaching, tutoring
> commission sales work

I am sure that there are a hundred more jobs you can think of that are appropriate to your abilities and circumstances. Sometimes, the best solution is starting your own *bootstrap* business and running it part time. Who knows — It may develop into something really big and surpass your salaried job. There are many possibilities.

Years ago, I couldn't find *any* job, so I bought some equipment and set out to clean chimneys. I was a chimney sweep! I didn't even have a Yellow Pages listing. All of my business came from knocking on doors and from word of mouth. I earned nearly $1,000 in my first full week!

The following is a partial list of businesses that can be started for little or nothing:

> chimney sweep
> typing service
> answering service
> delivery and light hauling service
> messenger service, singing telegrams, etc.
> lawn care
> house painter
> research service
> garage sales, flea market seller or promoter

cookie vendor
party promoter

Two of these businesses stand out for their *easy* profit. Both can net $750 to $1,000 a week if done properly! A description of both follows.

## How to Be a Cookie Vendor

What costs about 10 cents to make, but sells better than hot cakes for 50 cents or $1 each? *Homemade* chocolate chip cookies, oatmeal cookies, carrot cake, etc., all sell like crazy.

Come up with a *theme* that will attract both children and adults. Your theme could embody the name of your business, your logo, and your image, all rolled up into one. An example, which you can use if you wish, is the name "The Cookie Monster", a loveable beast who just loves to eat cookies. An appropriate rendition of your loveable monster can be drawn for you by an artist. Next, look into a variety of cookbooks and try out recipes until you have found the very best recipes that you can find. Later in this section, I have included my favorite recipes for chocolate chip cookies and carrot cake. Try them and compare them with your own.

The next step is to go to your busiest indoor shopping mall and arrange to rent space for a cookie booth right in the middle of the promenade. The mall manager will help you choose a location. A more complicated but versatile alternative is to construct a three-wheeled cart with fold-out trays and a large storage cabinet. Garden Way Stores offer a very well-balanced garden cart that can be adapted to your purpose.

If you choose to stay in one location, you may be able to set up a temporary cookie shop consisting of a chair, cash register, signs, and four long folding tables. You should have a three-dimensional "Cookie Monster" in the center, with signs facing pedestrian traffic. A large board should proclaim "BAKED FRESH DAILY" and display what you are selling, along with the price list. Plexiglass covers should protect your cookies from pilferage and flying insects. Wrap each cookie or slice of cake individually in plastic wrap. You could have two sizes — a regular cookie priced at 50 cents and a giant size for $1. How often you set up is determined by you, but Friday afternoon and evening and all day Saturday are good starting points.

Promotion and advertising are the keys to success in any business, including this one. Run a Grand Opening 1¢ sale on the opening Friday and Saturday. Ideally, you could hire someone to wear a "Cookie Monster" suit, which you will have to design and construct. Your "Cookie Monster" will hand out cookies for 1¢ each (one to a customer) to all comers.

Announce the big event a week before and then a day before the Grand Opening. Send a well-written, concise human interest story about you and your "Cookie Monster" business to the local newspapers, along with a picture of your "Cookie Monster" eating your delicious cookies. Perhaps you could even bake a gigantic cookie for him. The $200 or $300 it costs you to practically give your cookies away will bring in thousands of dollars worth of new business and public attention.

If you are thinking that this is a Mickey Mouse excuse for a business, think again! A woman in New York City began selling cookies inside a department store. Now, she is franchising a multimillion dollar cookie business all over the United States. A couple sold their homemade carrot cake to a few selected restaurants in Los Angeles. Today, they sell their carrot cake to 20,000 "7-11" stores from coast to coast. The recipes for chocolate chip cookies and carrot cake follow.

### Chocolate Chip Cookies

Cream together 1 cup brown sugar with 1 cup vegetable shortening.

Beat in 2 eggs.

Add in sequence 2 tablespoons water with ¾ teaspoon baking soda dissolved in it, ½ teaspoon vanilla, 2 cups flour, 1 large bag chocolate chips, and 2 cups oatmeal (optional).

Mix thoroughly.

Drop onto cookie sheets.

Bake at 350° F for 8 to 10 minutes.


### Carrot Cake

Blend 2 cups sugar, 4 eggs, and 1½ cups oil.

Add in sequence 2 cups flour, 2 teaspoons baking soda, 2 teaspoons baking powder, 2 teaspoons cinnamon, and 1 teaspoon salt.

Add 3 cups ground raw carrots and ½ cup walnuts (optional).

Mix thoroughly.

Bake at 350° F for 45 minutes in a greased 13" pan.


### Frosting for Cake

Beat together an 8 oz. package of cream cheese, softened, 1 stick of margarine, softened, 1 box of confectioners' sugar, and 1 teaspoon vanilla.

Spread on cooled cake.

## Business Party Promotion

Would you like to make a quick $750 to $1,000 a week helping other people promote their businesses? Hold weekly business and professional "Get to Meet Them" parties. In every town and city of reasonable size, there are attorneys eager to meet potential business clients, doctors looking for smart investment analysts, shop owners and small business owners wanting to meet bankers and investors. By holding a weekly informal get-together for business and professional people only, you can do your community a service and earn a handsome profit while you're at it.

You start out by contacting the owner of a popular nightclub to find out which is his slowest night. Offer to hold your business party for 250 of the top business people at his establishment. Charge $8 to $10 per customer. Split the admission fee right down the middle with the proprietor. He, of course, charges the usual amount for drinks. A week before, run a small display ad on the business page of your local newspaper. It could look something like this:

**CLUB NEW ENGLAND IS SPONSORING**
*Every Tues Night!!* **BUSINESSMEN'S PARTY** *Every Tues Night!!*

TOP BUSINESS PEOPLE AND PROFESSIONALS
WANTED FOR BUSINESS PARTY

This is your chance to meet bankers, attorneys, millionaire investors, real estate tycoons, CIA agents, accountants, venture capitalists, store owners, IBM exec's, rich entrepreneurs, fashion models. Limited to 500 of our top business leaders.

Business card and $10.00 required for admission at door. Reserve your personal invitation now by sending just $8.00 to

**CALL 861-1212**
**BUSINESS & PLEASURE Company**
1266 North Avenue, Burlington, VT 05401
'Business & Professional Ladies Free'

Bring plenty of cash and a lockable change box to the party in order to make change. Give each customer a stick-on name tag saying

MY NAME IS _____ .

MY BUSINESS IS _____ .

You may want to encourage eligible young ladies to attend by offering them free admission when you are first getting started. Soon, word of mouth advertising will build your party into the IN SPOT to be on that particular night of the week. You should easily net $750 to $1,000 each week using this plan!

## Borrow Money

The fourth seed money alternative is to borrow money. You can borrow from friends and relatives, but you must be willing to put up the largest amount of the stake yourself. If you don't believe in your project enough to take out a second mortgage on your home or to invest your life's savings, why should a friend, relative, or stranger risk his money? So, before approaching others, exhaust your own personal resources. Quite frankly, before borrowing, you should work the other three steps to exhaustion first. If you still cannot raise enough cash or if timing is critical, borrow what you need.

Evaluate your assets first. Do you own your own home? Can you take out a second mortgage loan? If possible, borrow against some of your assets by pledging them as collateral for a loan. Whole life insurance policies accumulate loan value after they have been in force for at least five years. This is a low interest loan.

Banks will usually grant a loan if your credit rating is good. If not, you **MUST** raise $500 using Steps 1, 2, and 3 given above. Deposit this money into a savings account at your bank. Now, apply for a personal-signature loan at your bank, using your savings account balance as collateral. Take the loan proceeds from your first bank, say $500, and open another account at another bank. Several days later, apply for a loan of $500, secured by your savings account. Repeat this process at three to eight more banks. When you've received your $500 loan from the last bank, deposit it into a checking account at one of the banks. Several days later, begin making payments towards the loans in all the banks. As you make the payments, a corresponding amount is released from its position as collateral in your savings accounts. Transfer this money from each savings account to your checking account, and continue to pay off your loans each week. By the end of sixty days or so, you will have paid off all your loans and have A-1 credit at ten banks.

IMPORTANT! When you open your first account, don't just walk in off the street and ask to open a new account. Always call first and set up an appointment to discuss opening up a new account. Come armed with business cards and a financial statement if you have one (or can have one made up).

## Raise $100,000 Within 24 Hours

Once you have established A-1 credit at ten banks, you are ready for phase two, which continues to build your credit to the level of the average millionaire Phase two takes about a year to accomplish, but by that time, you will be able to raise up to $100,000 within 24 hours just by signing. Here is how.

Sometime after establishing your credit at ten banks, go back to each one and request a $1,000 signature loan. When asked the purpose of this loan, it is usually best to mention home improvement, money for a much-needed vacation, or for school expenses for your kids (if appropriate). It is your right to change your mind after the loan is granted. What you actually do with the money is your business, as long as you pay it back as scheduled. Bankers do seem to give more weight to more frivolous uses of their money, such as vacationing with it, than to more (but risky) uses, like starting a new business. At any rate, a $1,000 signature loan is sure to be granted to a good customer like yourself who pays back his debts promptly. Get this $1,000 for 30 days. Deposit the loan proceeds, $10,000, (ten banks at $1,000 each) in one of your bank's checking accounts — pick one with a NOW interest-bearing account. The interest earned will help defray the loan interest cost. On the 30th day, promptly pay off each loan.

A month or so later, repeat the process, except this time apply for $3,000 or $5,000 — whatever you think they will lend you, and ask for a 60 day term note. Don't touch the money other than to deposit it into your NOW account. Again, promptly pay back each loan on the 60th day.

A couple of months later, repeat this process, this time requesting $10,000 at each of your ten banks. With your sterling repayment record, they can hardly refuse. This time around, your loan can be for 90 to 120 days. You have now established a $100,000 line of personal credit.

The bottom line to banks is whether you, their customer, pay them back with interest in a timely fashion. Once you have demonstrated this ability to their satisfaction, they couldn't care less that your W-2 form shows an annual income of $12,000, yet you are borrowing $10,000 at each bank.

Use the funds wisely and only for tested, viable money-making operations. You will never again have to pass up those special opportunities to double or triple your money because of insufficient funds.

If you don't like to deal with banks, you can deal with one of the loan by mail companies. Some of these firms will make unsecured loans of up to $30,000 by mail with little or no investigation. Most require you to have a stable financial history. A partial listing follows:

Avco Colorado Ind. Bank
P.O. Box 31225
Los Angeles, CA 90031

Finance America
2917 S. Western Ave.
Oklahoma City, OK 73109

C.II.T. Financial Corp.
650 Madison Ave.
New York, NY 10022

Bankers Investment Co.
Bankers Investment Bldg.
Hutchinson, KS 67501

Diversified Financial Corp. Ltd.
1145 Reservoir Ave.
Cranston, RI 02920
(401) 943-7551

Beneficial Executive Loan
   Service
2858 Stevens Creek Blvd.
San Jose, CA 95128

Dial Finance Corp.
2007 S. Main St.
P.O. Box 2321
Santa Ana, CA 92717

Nationwide Finance Corp.
Suite 927
1660 S. Albion St.
Denver, CO 80222

Postal Thrift Loans
703 Couglas St.
Sioux City, Iowa 51102

If you require $10,000 or more start-up capital, a Venture Capital firm can provide the funds. In return, they generally want a lucrative business plan and a share in the profits. These firms are highly selective. They are looking for the IBM's and the Xerox's of the future. They expect to triple or quadruple their investment in several years.

Applying for venture capital requires that you submit a business plan. This is best prepared by a professional, a financial advisor, a business advisor, or a business promoter. It should project all aspects of your business for three years. Contacting any of the Venture Capital firms listed can give you information on what is required. An extensive list of firms with money to lend follows:

Arthur Anderson & Company
69 W. Washington Street
Chicago, IL 60602

Advance Growth Capital Corp.
401 Madison St.
Maywood, IL 60153

Johns Hollensbe & Assoc.
4126 Pleasantdale Rd.
Suite B-227
Atlanta, GA 30340

All State Venture Capital Corp.
Box 5008
Westport, CT 06880

Bayside Capital Corp.
706 One Main Plaza E.
Norfolk, VA 23510

Hellman, Gal & Co.
One Federal St.
Boston, MA 02110

Irving Capital Corp.
One Wall Street
New York, NY 10005

United Capital Corp. of Ill.
State & Wyman Streets
Rockford, IL 61101

Merril Lynch, Pierce, Fenner,
& Smith, Inc.
Two Penn Plaza
New York, NY 10001

Continental Capital Corp.
Bank of America Center
San Francisco, CA 94104

Winston-Walker Enterprises
3491 Ingleside Road
Shaker Heights, OH 44122

Washington Capital Corp.
P.O. Box 1770
Seattle, WA 98111

Avco Corp.
1275 King
Greenwich, CT 06930

Cameron-Brown Capital Corp.
Box 18109
Raleigh, NC 27609

General Research Corp.
5383 Hollister Ave.
Santa Barbara, CA 93111

Harvey Brooks and Company
1251 Ave. of the Americas
New York, NY 10020

Brittany Capital Corp.
4325 R.N.B. Tower
Dallas, TX 75201

Royal Street Investment Corp.
521 Royal Street
New Orleans, LA 70130

Gold Coast Capital Corp.
3550 Biscayne Boulevard
Miami, FL 33137

Euclid Partners
50 Rockefeller Plaza
New York, NY 10020

Union Venture Corporation
445 South Figueroa Street
Los Angeles, CA 90017

Alison Promotions
5834 Soledad Mt. Rd.
La Jolla, CA 92307

Opportunity Capital Corp.
680 Beach Street, Suite 311
San Francisco, CA 94109

Investors Capital Corp.
144 Golden Hill Street
  Suite 525
Bridgeport, CT 06604

Small Business Investment
  Company of Hawaii, Inc.
1575 South Berentania Street
Honolulu, HI 96814

Vermont Investment Capital,
  Inc.
Rt. 14
South Royalton, VT 05608

M & T Capital Corp.
One M & T Plaza
Buffalo, NY 14240

Innoven Capital Corp.
Park 80 Plaza West One
Saddle Brook, NJ 07662

Arcata Investment Co.
2750 Sand Hill Road
Menlo Park, CA 94025

Heizer Corp.
20 N. Wacher Ave.
Chicago, IL 60601

Fidelity Venture Associates
35 Congress Street
Boston, MA 02110

Basic Equities, Inc.
P.O. Box 1207
Easton, MD 21601

Financial Resources
2211 Sterick Bldg.
Memphis, TN 38103

Kleiner, Perkins, Caulfield, and
  Byers
#2 Embarcadero Square
San Francisco, CA

Matrix Venture Funds, Inc.
710 N. Plankinton Ave.
Suite 622
Milwaukee, WI 53203

First Investment Corp. of
  Chicago
One First National Plaza
Chicago, IL 60670

CSC Capital Corporation
1800 Mercantile Dallas Bldg.
Dallas, TX 75201

Moramerica Capital Corp.
200 American Bldg.
Cedar Rapids, IA 52401

Massachusetts Capital Corp.
111 Devonshire Street
Boston, MA 02109

Financial Consultants
P.O. Box 297
Uniontown, KY 42461

Vanguard Capital Corp.
120 S. LaSalle Street
Chicago, IL 60603

MESBIC Financial Corp.
   of Dallas
P.O. Box 6228
Dallas, TX 75222

Memorial Drive Trust
25 Acorn Park
Cambridge, MA 02140

First Texas Investment Co.
13025 Champions Drive
Houston, TX 77069

Enervest, Inc.
5500 S. Syracuse Circle,
   Suite 269
Englewood, CO 80110

Harvey Brooks and Company
35 Executive Park Drive
Atlanta, GA 30329

First Heartland, Inc.
Box 463
Austin, MN 55912

George D. Poe and Co.
913 Pacific Ave.
Tacoma, WA 94802

First Piedmont Capital Corp.
P.O. Box 3028
Greenville, SC 29602

Hercules, Inc.
910 Market Street
Wilmington, DE 19899

# CHAPTER 5
# The Five Little Known Principles for Amassing Wealth

As I said in Chapter 1, virtually all money is made by **selling** something. That something can be labor, professional services, royalty rights, merchandise, or the use of something, such as an apartment or money in the bank.

There are three ingredients to any sale: 1. the product itself, 2. the customer or purchaser, and 3. the marketing of that product. We are concerned here only with the selling of a product, such as merchandise, information, or ideas. Why? Because no matter who you are or from where you are starting, you *can* acquire and market merchandise, information, and ideas.

> WEALTH PRINCIPLE #1: **Of the three ingredients to any sale, the marketing of the product is far more important than the product itself.**

Even a grocery store, which sells the most necessary staple of life, food, succeeds or fails according to how it markets its products, rather than on the products themselves. The buyer must perceive that the food is better, more wholesome, and lower priced than anywhere else, or he will buy his food elsewhere.

Today's tomatoes, bright pink and uniformly round, are *inferior*, except in looks, to almost any tomato sold 40 years ago. You yourself can grow a far more delicious tomato at home in your own garden! Modern tomatoes are bred for uniform shape, not flavor. They are picked green, injected, and sprayed, so that when finally seen at the grocery store, they are all bright red and luscious looking. Marketing has proven that the consumer will buy the *appearance* of the perfect tomato in preference to the ungainly, but flavorful, varieties most home gardeners cherish.

Creative marketing can take a commonplace product which is sold everywhere and suddenly make it sell fantastically better than previously! Three Harvard students decided to market records and tapes on television by showing videos of top music groups and adding a catchy and memorable toll-free order number, 1-800-HOT-ROCK. The idea is insanely simple, yet the business is quadrupling annually!

WEALTH PRINCIPLE #2: **Sell something that results in multiple, continuous sales, yielding high profits with little effort.**

Choose your product carefully. If you are starting with little or no resources and still want to make huge profits, information, books, and ideas are the most lucrative product available to you.

Information costs you nothing more than the time and effort required to do the research or to set your own ideas down on paper. Ideas are **free** and are available to anybody with a creative imagination. A creative imagination is something you will acquire as you develop your *Mind for Success*. Do not think that this is impossible just because you have never "created" anything before. Truly fundamental and radical innovations are few and far between. Most new ideas are either small improvements on existing ideas or the combination of existing ideas in a slightly different way.

The finished product, information, is merely printed paper, in the form of a book, pamphlet, manual, or, possibly, a tape. A large printer can "manufacture" your product in large quantities for pennies a copy. People purchase your product because they are sold by your advertising and because the information received is **useful** to them. They couldn't care less that the actual cost of the paper and printing is just 50¢ or less, as long as the information on the paper satisfies a desire or need.

**Direct marketing of INFORMATION provides the largest profit markup of any business I know.**

If you singlehandedly create and sell your product, information, you have successfully purchased your product at the cheapest possible wholesale price (from the source) and have sold it for the highest possible retail markup in business! You have also eliminated the middleman. Markups range from ten to thirty times your cost. These profits are all yours to keep, after taxes, of course.

Fortunes have been made by selling other products via *direct mail advertising,* but why settle for a 4 to 6 times markup when you could make up to *30* times your cost? Why worry about buying and stocking quantities of merchandise necessary to maintain inventory?

If you are selling information, ten thousand dollars' worth of inventory costs you less than $700 at your local printer. Paperback books and folios are easy to store and easy to ship. Many printers are willing to store your inventory in return for a large order. This is how it works. Let's say that you have written a manual and have had it typeset. Your printer agrees to print 2,000 copies at $2 each. Your initial sales campaign enables you to sell all 2,000 copies at $10 each. This test of your manual and your advertising campaign was successful, and you project that you should be able to sell 15,000 more copies during the course of the coming year. At $2 a copy, that would cost you $30,000 for inventory alone! Negotiate with your printer. Tell him that you will order 15,000 more manuals, but that you need his best, most competitive, price. Check around. The price for 15,000 units should get down to between 55¢ and 65¢ a copy. Tell him that you will place your order with him if he will store your books at no charge until sold.

Most printers will readily accept this proposition if you agree to pay for the initial 4,000 or so at the old price of $2 a copy. This way, the printer recovers his out of pocket expenses and is more willing to wait for payment on the balance. He has recovered $8,000 with the first 4,000 manuals delivered. He can easily afford to wait for the $1,750 balance (15,000 x 65¢ is $9,750). This also helps you out later in the year, when your cost per copy drops to an effective rate of 16¢ each ($1,750 divided by the remaining 11,000 copies).

Other products you can sell that are based on information as a commodity are tapes, records, computer programs, pictures, and photographs. Each of these cost little to reproduce once the original is finished. Each of these is easily shipped and stored. Each of these products can be sold for 10 to 30 times their actual cost. If writing a book frightens you, consider the other types of information-related products one by one. I cannot emphasize too strongly that:

**Direct marketing of information-related products is the most profitable business enterprise available today.**

Even if you presently have $100,000 or more starting capital, you cannot find a more lucrative business opportunity! For those starting with $5,000 or less, self-publishing is the surest route to wealth. How to create and market these information-related products will be examined in the following chapters.

WEALTH PRINCIPLE #3: **Follow up sales of your first product with sales of related product(s) to the same customers.**

In direct marketing, these are called *backend* or *bounceback* offers. They are crucial to your long-range success. The reason is simple. No single product you are likely to come up with will have a permanent market. Securing your customers costs you plenty. You must pay for advertising space or rent hundreds of names to secure just one customer.

To resell to that same customer on a bounceback offer costs you practically nothing. Virtually all successful direct marketers enclose a new ad with each product they deliver. As many as 20% of the original customers will immediately order a second different, but related, product. Taken to its ultimate conclusion, not just one, but several, can be offered — in a catalogue. Catalogue selling is one of the fastest-growing and most profitable techniques open to the direct marketer today. For example, The Sharper Image sells all kinds of upbeat, high fashion jewelry, gadgets, and tools available almost nowhere else. They promote a volume-selling product through effective space ads in magazines and newspapers. With thousands of new customers in hand, they deliver the original product ordered plus their latest catalogue — and reap thousands of dollars more in backend sales.

Were you to sell a diet book, you might follow up with a nutritive diet supplement or vitamins. An example of the projected profit figures follows. Let us say that you are marketing a diet book that sells for $10 each and costs 75¢ each to print in quantity. One direct mail campaign, sending advertisements to 100,000 names, results in the sale of 5,000 books.

*Sales*

| | | |
|---|---|---|
| 5,000 books @ $10 | = | $50,000 |

*Expenses*

| | | |
|---|---|---|
| Cost of books | | |
| (5,000 @ $.75) | = | $ 3,750 |
| Cost to rent mailing list | | |
| (100,000 names @ $65/1,000) | = | $ 6,500 |
| Cost to print brochures | | |
| (100,000 @ 5.7¢) | = | $ 5,700 |
| Postage for 100,000 brochures | | |
| (100,000 @ $.11, bulk rate) | = | $11,000 |
| Cost of mailing service | | |
| (100,000 @ $19/1,000) | = | $ 1,900 |
| Cost to ship orders | | |
| (5,000 @ $1.05) | = | $ 5,250 |
| Cost to refund 10% of all orders | | |
| (500 @ $10) | = | $ 5,000 |
| Total Expenses | = | $39,100 |

*Profit from Mailing*

| | | |
|---|---|---|
| Total sales | = | $50,000 |
| Total expenses | = | $39,100 |
| Profit | = | $10,900 |

A profit of $10,900 is not a bad income for 2 months' easy work. However, the picture can be considerably improved by sending a small catalogue along with each book order. This catalogue is included at no extra cost for postage and advertises nutritional products, such as vitamin supplements. Assume that the cost of printing this catalogue is $.22 each. Assume that 20% of your original diet book customers order an average of $30 worth of products, that 10% reorder more catalogue products to replace what they have consumed at an average reorder of $20, and that your markup is 200%. A markup of 200% means that you charge the customer 3 times what the product costs you. You also charge 10% for shipping. Our profit picture has just changed dramatically!

*Sales from Catalogue*

| | | |
|---|---|---|
| Catalogue orders | | |
| (1,000 @ $30) | = | $30,000 |
| Catalogue reorders | | |
| (500 @ $20) | = | $10,000 |
| Shipping charged to customer | | |
| (10% of sales) | = | $ 4,000 |
| **Total Sales** | = | **$44,000** |

*Expenses for the New Sales*

| | | |
|---|---|---|
| Cost of catalogues | | |
| (5,000 @ $.22) | = | $ 1,100 |
| Cost of product | | |
| (1/3 of sales) | = | $13,333 |
| Cost of shipping | = | $ 4,000 |
| **Total Expenses** | = | **$18,433** |

*Profit from New Sales*

| | | |
|---|---|---|
| Total Sales | = | $44,000 |
| Total Expenses | = | $18,433 |
| **Profit** | = | **$25,567** |

The extra sales from your catalogue orders has

given you $25,567 in **additional** profit with virtually no additional effort. Your catalogue sales increased your total profit to three times that obtained from the original mailing. Your total net income is about $32,600 over a three month period as the result of a single mailing.

After a month or two, catalogues can be mailed to all 5,000 original book customers, and sales will continue. With a consumable product, such as vitamins or diet supplements, customers will continue to re-order, sometimes for years. It is this customer file of repeat, steady buyers that becomes a perpetual goldmine.

> WEALTH PRINCIPLE #4: **Delegate 90% of the operation of your business to skilled professionals, then compound profits by inter-related expansion.**

At this juncture, your first enterprise is successful, and better than 90% self-sufficient. You must hire others to take over the daily grind. As you become

*File 100 orders a day, pack 'em & ship 'em!*

truly successful, you will be able to attract others with the talents and skills you may lack to join your business. Provide an incentive plan for your key people. Reward them for increasing your profits with a share of those profits. Employees can and should do everything but provide the creative imagination necessary for *new* projects. This is your bailiwick; it is what *you* do best.

Think of each new project that you start as a conduit for the flow of wealth. Ideally, each enterprise should require no more from you personally than a water main requires of the homeowners who use it. Yet the combined force of numerous conduits flowing together can be substantial.

In the business world, these money-making conduits are called **vehicles**. A vehicle is any investment, patent, title, copyright, or business that when owned and promoted generates income for its owner. The ideal vehicle generates substantial ongoing income with virtually no labor input by the owner. For example, twenty years ago, the singer Andy Williams recorded his version of "Moon River". Today, it is *still* selling 25,000 records a month. Mr. Williams' only involvement at this time is to deposit his monthly royalty check.

A somewhat less satisfactory vehicle is apartment rentals. Owning just one apartment can cause a lot of headaches for the amount of return. Owning ten or more units results in *"Economies of Scale"* that begin to make income property a satisfactory vehicle. Each additional unit in the same complex raises the income with little proportionate increase in the fixed costs. With ten or more units, the landlord may be able to afford to hire an apartment manager and avoid expending much of his own time and labor.

55

By combining diverse but inter-related money-making vehicles, you can create an ongoing stream of income requiring little of your personal time and labor.

Just as you can acquire someone else's discarded automobiles and restore them to good working order, so can you acquire other people's cast-off income-producing vehicles and restore them to full income-producing order.

I know of two 25 year old inventions on which the patents have expired which are based on principles of human psychology. When combined with today's personal computers, the result is a program that could revolutionize learning and personal motivation. The coalescing of these ideas into a patentable program may result in a *million dollar vehicle*. In case you're wondering — I'm working on it. This concept illustrates the underlying principle behind *Mind Over Money*.

**The combination of creative imagination with active research is the most potent resource available to you. Just one *idea* followed by *action* can provide you with a million dollar vehicle.**

Ideas and unused vehicles abound. Often, the original creator of a vehicle lacked the necessary promotional skills needed to turn a great idea into a money-making reality. In some cases, the inventor stopped just short of success. A simple adjustment here and there could turn failure to success.

WEALTH PRINCIPLE #5:  **Treat businesses like products — Buy them low and sell them high.**

Once you have created a self-sustaining, profit-making enterprise, it will reach a point where it could be sold for many times its out of pocket cost to you. Let's say that a business in which you invested $100,000 now nets $150,000 annually. A buyer appears, waving a million dollars plus a piece of stock in the parent company. Should you sell out? Sure, if the price is right. Starting and selling businesses ultimately could multiply your wealth many times over.

The latest ploy is to have your cake and eat it too by *going public*. You offer stock in your business to the public, while holding back some of the stock for yourself. Going public inflates the valuation of your company overnight and lets entrepreneurs sell a small portion of their holdings for major returns. Allen Paulson waited fifteen years to go public, and now he is $90 million richer. Paulson formed American Jet, Inc., in 1967, and, by 1981, he had created Gulfstream Aerospace Corp. to run his newly streamlined aircraft manufacturing operation. When Gulfstream went public in April, 1983, its 1982 revenues had been $582 million, with earnings of $43 million. Gulfstream's book value soared from $31.9 million to $637 million. The stock offering raised $167.2 million. Paulson himself sold 4.75 million shares of his own stock, reducing his equity from 95.8% to 73.7% and netting him an incredible $90 million.

The five basic wealth-building principles just outlined are used by most self-made wealthy people. They can take you from an insignificant amount of seed capital to $90,000,000 cash, just as they did for Allen Paulson.

# CHAPTER 6
# Starting Your Own Business

Because selling information-related products via direct mailing (mail-order) is, in my opinion, your surest shot at success, that is the type of business we will discuss. Once you have mastered this business and want to diversify, you will find that business principles are pretty much the same.

You can begin by choosing a quiet place in your home in which to work. If you have a spare bedroom, convert it into your office. Other locations are fine, as long as you can work without interruption for several hours at a time. Furnish your new office with the basics. Start with a desk or writing table and chair. A file cabinet will soon become indispensable for organizing correspondence, work in progress, receipts, etc. Lacking that, you can make do with a fiberboard filing box, available at large office supply firms. You will need a typewriter — either manual or electric is fine. Professionals type all correspondence, so get used to the idea. You will soon need storage cabinets or shelving (in a dry location) for storing books, stationery, forms, etc. Lease a postage meter from Pitney-Bowes. Eventually, you will need a computer with a list management program.

In the direct marketing field, you can at first get by with an extension of your home telephone. Later, you should have a separate business number, which will give you a listing in the yellow pages. The use of a toll-free 800 number is a future option that will enhance your marketing once you generate a large enough volume to justify it.

## Choosing a Name

Use your own name or choose a business name. Often, it is best simply to do business in your own name, such as Charles Scribner, Publisher. Some names sound good with a possessive "s" added. Harrold Lippa becomes "Lippa's". A shorter, catchier name is better than an elaborate one. The Gold Exchange is better than Hudson Valley Precious Metals, Inc. Advertising space costs money, and a simple catchy name is easier to remember. Choose a name that is distinctive, but appealing. Slobobovitz Publishing doesn't make it as a pleasing business name. Hamilton House is fine.

Once you have chosen your DBA (doing business as) name, you must register it. The process is simple. Fill out forms obtained from your state Attorney General's office, and send them in along with the required nominal fee. You should also register with your local county clerk. They may require you to run a "DBA" announcement in the local newspaper. If nobody else has pre-empted your name or one similar enough to be confusing, you will be duly registered. The primary reason for registering with the state is not to protect your business name and logo, but to protect the consumer, who needs to know the identity of the owner. You can write to the U.S. Patent & Trademark Office to protect a trademark. Write to:

Assistant Secretary & Commissioner of Patents
   & Trademarks
Patent & Trademark Office
Washington, DC 20231
703-557-3158

You should consider stylizing your business name by a distinctive type face or a specially designed logo. IBM is always advertised in distinctive block letters. That is the only trademark they need. You can do the same by contacting a professional typesetter or advertising agency, who will show you numerous styles of type available and/or design a logo for your business. Once this is done, take your camera-ready graphics to a printer and have several hundred or more sheets of 8½ by 11" business letterheads and envelopes printed. At the same time, order 500-1,000 business cards.

If you really want to professionalize your image, open a business checking account, and have your logo imprinted on your new blue or grey business-sized checks. Ask the printer to begin with a high check number, such as 3,000. This will give your business that already well-established look.

For record-keeping, we use the Chek-Matic System provided by New England Business Services (Telephone toll-free 1-800-225-6380 for their catalogue.). The Chek-Matic System allows you to itemize all expenses and deposits into categories, all on the same sheet. You can keep complete records as you go along, each time you write a check or enter a deposit. Bookkeeping is as simple as balancing your checkbook and totalling each category.

## Legal Aspects

Once you have registered your business name,

there are no licenses or permits required for a publishing or mail-order business. Even the local zoning for your house can be residential, rather than commercial, as long as all of your sales activity is done through the mails.

If you plan to sell products within your own state, you will probably need to register to collect sales tax. Request the proper forms through the appropriate agency. Each state bureaucracy has its own euphemism or "bureaucratise" for the sales tax agency. They may call it the State Board Of Equalization, the State Department of Taxes, or something else altogether. Ask your state's information office for assistance.

## Record Keeping

It is an absolute **must** to keep accurate records. Good recordkeeping is necessary, both to provide quality customer service and to save you money when tax time comes. If you work out of your home, you can deduct that portion of your home's mortgage, utilities, and taxes that corresponds to the space you use for business and only for business. If a portion of your home is used both for business and living, you cannot take the deduction for that portion. Deduct costs of your business telephone (or that portion of your home telephone used for business). Deduct *all* business-related expenses, ranging from office supplies, furniture, and postage to an automobile used for business. You may lease equipment, such as an electric typewriter, postage meter, computer with printer, and your business vehicle. Deduct all of these leasing expenses from income when filling out your tax return.

Running your own business is the first step

toward attaining great wealth because it allows you to shelter a large income from the ravages of taxes to a far greater degree than is possible to the salaried employee. As a self-employed businessperson, you can establish a healthcare plan for you and your family plus your employees, if any, and deduct its cost. You can deduct the cost of any business-related travel. Travel to Hawaii to visit a client or attend a business seminar, and deduct the entire cost of the trip! You can put aside up to 15% of your income, up to $15,000 annually for your retirement under the Keogh Plan. This investment money is deducted from your taxable income, often at a great savings in taxes.

## Business Organization

You can choose to do business as an individual in a sole proprietorship. You can join forces with another person to form a partnership, or you can form your own corporation.

Working for yourself in your own business has numerous benefits, not the least of which are the tax savings just mentioned. Its great advantage is simplicity. Forming a sole proprietorship business is as simple as registering your business name, opening a business checking account at your bank, and having stationery and business cards printed. As a sole proprietor, you personally are the president, treasurer, secretary, and sales force. You, and you only, are accountable.

## Partnership

If one person has money and another has ideas, energy, and knowledge, it is tempting to put the two together. Just keep in mind that any time you accept money for a piece of your business, you are giving up autonomy and a share of the profits. When you borrow from an individual or institution, stick to a loan wherein you are obligated only for the loan principle plus interest. That way, when you are successful, you can pay off the loan and write off the interest as a business expense.

Two people with complementary assets, whether in skills or finances, may combine to form a winning team. For example, an experienced writer and a direct marketing expert could team up and do better than either one alone. It comes down to personal judgement to decide whether giving up half the profits (and possibly saving half the effort) is worth it. I would guess that as many partnerships have failed because of partnership conflicts than from any other single reason.

Be sure to have an agreement in writing at the inception of your joint venture, and be sure to have an attorney review your partnership agreement. This is crucial, since you personally are equally liable for any debts, obligations, or legal violations your partner incurs in the course of business. When a partner dies, the other may suddenly have to buy out his partner's share in order to settle the estate.

## Corporation

A corporation is defined as an artificial being, a legal entity, capable of carrying out all legal and business transactions as though it were a single individual. A corporation is usually, but not always, composed of an association of individuals acting as a unit or single individual for a common purpose. A corporation is ongoing. That is, it continues to exist and function regardless of changes in its individual membership.

The benefits of incorporating are:

1. Personal liability of owners is limited to their capital contribution for stock payments.
2. Transfer of ownership, whether total or partial, is easily arranged by transferring shares. Stock is easily sold.
3. Employees and owners of a corporation can easily participate in pension and profit-sharing plans, group health insurance plans, and incentive programs with stock options. In many cases, the taxable costs of these programs is less than in other business forms.
4. If an owner dies, the corporation lives on, and does not have to be liquidated for probate.
5. Corporations can raise money they never have to pay back by issuing shares of stock. A closely held corporation (shares limited to just a few people) can go public. The owner can often recoup his equity and sometimes a large profit without giving up or selling a controlling interest in his business.
6. There are tax advantages via pension funds, sheltering income, and deductions for business losses that are not available to sole proprietorships and partnerships.

To form your own corporation, write to the Secretary of State in your state, requesting all necessary forms and a schedule of fees. An excellent book on the subject is *How to Form Your Own Corporation* from the Citizens Law Library by Harper Hamilton Press, Inc., 4720 Hancock Drive, Boulder, CO 80303.

## Laws That Affect Your Business

Three agencies are concerned with your business. These are:

## Federal Trade Commission:
## "The mail-order merchandise rule"

The FTC has a rule that protects the mail-order shopper. According to the mail-order rule adopted in October, 1975,

1. You must deliver merchandise when you say you will.
2. If you don't specify a delivery date, you must ship merchandise no later than 30 days after receiving an order.
3. The customer has the right to cancel his order for a refund if the merchandise is not received shortly after the 30 day period.

If you can't comply with the specified delivery date, you must notify your customers of the delay and new shipping date. You must offer them the option of a refund and a postpaid envelope with which to respond. No response means that the customer has accepted the delay. If the customer will not accept the delay and asks for a refund, it must be sent by the end of the first 30 day delay.

Mail-order dealers used to test-market an item. If response was satisfactory, they would rush it into production. Today, you must have the product in-hand, ready for shipping, before you ever advertise. Be sure to follow this rule scrupulously. Not shipping on time because your printer was late, for instance, will cause you more headaches than I can list.

The FTC is also concerned with false or misleading advertising, fraudulent business practices, and unfair competition. If you make a statement in your advertising, be sure that you can substantiate it. Have an attorney review questionable sales literature before printing it, if in doubt.

## Better Business Bureau

Consumer complaints often wind up here. Visit the local office, and seek membership. Their assistance and backing can be invaluable.

## U.S. Postal Inspector

The far-reaching powers of the United States Postal Service are not something to take lightly. Two statutes affect the self publisher. The first is a *criminal* mail fraud statute, 18 U.S.C., Section 1341. The second is the *civil* "False Representation" Statute, 39 U.S.C., Section 3005.

The U.S. Postal Service has the authority to seek criminal prosecution for mail fraud. Penalties are up to a $1,000 fine or 5 years' imprisonment *per violation*. Due process must be followed, i.e., a charge is heard before a proper independent judge/jury, and the Post Office is required to prove mail fraud.

The civil statute is more intimidating. The False Representation Statute allows the U.S. Postal Service to destroy a business or suppress a product or book it doesn't like by issuing a "mail stop order". The defendant's incoming mail is seized and stamped with the defamatory message that the addressee has violated the False Representation Statute. All incoming mail is then returned to the sender. In effect, the defendant's business is destroyed, since all income is cut off. This is done *without* the customary due process.

The U.S. Postal Service acts as complainant, prosecutor, judge, jury, appeals court, enforcement agency, precedent-setter, and, to a large degree, *lawmaker*! The U.S. Postal Service rules in favor of itself over 98% of the time at its own "kangaroo court" hearings. Filing an appeal of a U.S.P.S. judgement is futile. The process is convoluted, expensive, and biased against the defendant. With his incoming mail cut off, the defendant is deprived of all income and, thus, essentially fined up to thousands of dollars *before* a verdict is found.

The U.S.P.S. is now seeking even further-reaching powers with no additional due process protection for the accused. These new powers would include:

1. Power to issue its own Cease and Desist Orders.
2. Power to have its orders enforced with fines of up to $20,000 a day against businesses and persons.
3. *Authority to legally ban books!*
4. A mandate to conduct a consumer education program.
5. *Expanded* "punishment before hearing" authority.

Unfortunately, there are a whole array of new laws and proposed bills before Congress that have the effect of undermining our Constitutional rights in every area, not just in mail-order. A whole book could be written on *The Erosion of Constitutional Rights in America;* any takers out there?

## Copyright Laws

One law that protects you is the Copyright Law. Any book, pamphlet, page, or leaflet can be protected from unauthorized publication and sale by obtaining a copyright. Write to the U.S. Copyright Office, Library of Congress, Washington, DC 20559 to request forms. Before publishing your material, insert the appropriate copyright information on the title page in order to legally protect your work. By printing *copy-*

*right* © *the year and your name*, you are legally protected whether or not you have filed the proper forms with the U.S. Copyright Office. If you devise successful advertising copy, ads, sales letters, etc., you should also copyright this material.

# CHAPTER 7
# The Keys to Business Success — Advertising and Promotion

You would be hardpressed selling the greatest product in the world without enthusiastic, *inspired* advertising copy.

PRINCIPLE #1

Choose a dynamic "best-selling" topic first, then write inspired and powerfully-selling advertisements for it. Then develop the written product to live up to the advertisement.

A product should fill a human desire or need. Advertising copy is an exercise in appealing to *all* the desires and needs a product could arouse in a customer. By **first** exploring all those desires and needs that could make a product sell, a better product often results.

If you look at the top ten best-selling books in any given month, you will see three broad topic areas that are perennially there. These are: sex and romance; diet, health, and self-improvement; and money management and business. These topics are sure winners. A book on *Deciduous Trees Native to North America* will not find nearly the readership as the above topics, no matter how well it is written. It therefore makes good sense to choose a topic closely allied to these three basic human interests.

PRINCIPLE #2

> An advertisement has but one purpose, to make sales!

Fancy prose, intellectual virtuosity, humor, and high style have no place in an advertisement unless they demonstrably increase sales. Surprisingly, some of the most tasteless ads, especially on TV, pull the largest responses.

## Writing a Sales Letter

There are three main elements to an ad: headline, subcaption, and body copy. Of these, the headline is the most important. A headline must **stop** readers in their tracks and keep them from turning the page or tossing the ad into the wastebasket. A headline should appeal to the readers' self-interest, indicate potential benefits, relay news, and spark curiosity.

## How to Write a Powerful Headline

Use powerful, attention-grabbing words. The word "FREE", when appropriate is by far the most powerful word. Others are: "Revolutionary," "New," "Amazing," and "Easy." Also, large dollar amounts, such as $100,000 can often be quite effective. For example: "Amazing Device Discovers $100,000 in Gold for Inventor." This headline uses attention-grabbing words, "amazing," "$100,000," and "gold" to stop the reader cold. It is in a news format, which arouses curiosity for the rest of the story.

Use the words "How to" in order to arouse the readers' self-interest. Follow up with benefits. For example, "New Plan Reveals How to Safely Lose 25 Pounds a Week." Here is newsworthy information.

"How to" promises the reader possible benefits, especially if he is overweight.

Encourage the reader with how quickly or easily he can satisfy his desires. For example, "The Easiest, Quickest $100,000 You'll Ever Make" was the headline for a recent get-rich-quick pamphlet. A more powerful headline is hard to imagine. People are basically lazy; I know I am. If you can satisfy their desires without frightening them with the necessity for work, your ad will sell.

Offer the reader an engaging choice by asking "Which?". For example, "Which Young Lady is the Mother and Which One is the Daughter?" The prospect is led to guess on something that could be of interest to him.

Use the word "Why" to engage the readers' interest in newsworthy information. For example, "Why Work for a Living, When You Can Relax and Grow Rich?". This headline makes the reader stop and think. It fires his curiosity, making him wonder how it is possible to both relax and grow rich.

## When You Are About to Write an Ad, Fire Yourself Up

Build enthusiasm for the product. If the product is only in your mind, so much the better; imagine the best product possible. After you are suitably worked up, consciously relax. Don't worry about writing the perfect headline. Then, before you fall asleep, dream up one headline after another, using each of the techniques listed above. Jot down each idea as it comes to mind. Review the four motivators a headline should embody, and refine the best headlines until one or two stand out. Get help, if necessary, to narrow down the choice. Remember, the headline should inexorably pull the reader into the body of the ad. If your headline doesn't lead you naturally into the subheading, you cannot expect it to do so for the reader. **Important** — Always keep in mind what you and your product can do for the reader, **not** how the product relates to you.

One advertiser today has printed on his envelope and sales literature a picture of himself with the caption, "multimillionaire by age 29." Most readers don't want to hear about it! Frankly, it is aggravating to most of us, struggling to survive, to see a 29 year old youngster bragging of his success. More appealing would be a picture with a testimonial from a former customer: "This plan changed my life forever. I now own my own successful business, and I truly believe your plan can help anyone."

## Emotional Appeals Have Power Where Logic Fails

People will believe **anything** if it SATISFIES AN EMOTIONAL NEED. Stir up powerful emotional appeals first, then resort to logic to convert a skeptical reader into a buyer.

Purchase a copy of the *National Enquirer*. Better yet, buy several months' back issues. Examine the ads and find those that are repeated month after month. A full page ad in the *National Enquirer* costs in the neighborhood of $22,000. A successful space ad grosses two to five times its cost. You KNOW that if an ad is routinely repeated, it MUST be making money for the advertiser. Observe those ads that are repeated. Some of them have the poorest possible excuse for a product that you can imagine, yet they sell thousands each month!

One ad sold "Incan Worry Stones". These are stones polished for millions of years on the shores of the Amazon River. These stones could be used as a worry stone (Just rub it, and your worries dissolve), as a prayer stone (Hold it and meditate; it will help you communicate with God), or as a thinking stone (Don't make any serious decision without first taking the time to rub your thinking stone). Believe it or not, each stone sells for $3.95 or three for $10, plus $2 shipping.

If pebbles from the beach can be sold for $10 through emotional appeals, **anything** can be sold! Just one element of "logic" is enough to convince the reader that the appeal is genuine and that he should order. In this case, the ad stated, "These stones were highly prized by the Incas, who carried them for hundreds of years — one of the longest peaceful interludes in mankind's history. Think what they will do for you!".

## Subheading

**A powerful subheading excites the reader and leads him inexorably into the body copy.** The subheading is both a bridge and a motivator. It should clarify and amplify points in the headings. For example:

> HEADING: HOW YOU CAN MAKE HUGE
> PROFITS IN YOUR OWN PUBLISHING
> BUSINESS
> SUBHEADING: WITHOUT WRITING A BOOK
> ... OR ANYTHING AT ALL
> WITHOUT WRITING ANY ADVERTISING
> WITHOUT RISKING LARGE SUMS
> OF MONEY

This subheading clarifies the heading, builds curiosity, and leads directly into the body copy.

Another example:

HEADING: POLAR BEARS ARE BACK!

SUBHEADING: The spirit of those INDOMIT-
ABLE DENIZENS of the frozen North have
been captured in a LIFESIZE WORK OF ART.

PARALLEL HEADING: A POLAR BEAR RUG
OF ALL MAN-MADE MATERIALS

In this case, two headings are employed, with a link-
ing subheading leading into the body of the ad.

SECOND SUBHEADING: The ferocious head is
so realistic that you might have to muzzle your
dog, comfort your children, and pacify neighborhood conservationists!

## Body Copy

Before getting into the body of the ad, you
should decide which approach you will take. The
predominant type of ad for selling books shows a
picture of the book, and tells the reader what the book
is about and how it can benefit him. This is the objective approach. The ad flows in logical steps, backed
up by facts, to the conclusion that you should buy the
book offered.

Another type of ad is the subjective approach,
based on **emotion**. You sell the sizzle, not the steak.
Back up emotionally charged statements with testimonials from readers who have been helped. Don't tell
what the book is about as much as what using it can
do for you. Rather than say, "Chapter 6 has six medi-
cally approved exercises for strengthening the back,"
say, "In Chapter 6, you will learn how experts banish
lower back pain forever!".

The objective facts often lead to a newspaper
story type of format. You know the kind of ad that
doesn't look like an ad and that even has to have the

word "advertisement" printed at the top. This type is often effective because it doesn't look like an ad, and it seems to carry more credibility.

The public is continually bombarded with stri-

dent ads. Those that are too sensational to be realistic are simply glanced at and ignored. You can over-sell! People unconsciously think that if the advertiser is pushing so hard to sell the product, that it can't possibly be that good. If the ad is overly sensational, it loses legitimacy.

Good advertising is NOT harmonious, pleasant-appearing, and bland! On the contrary, the "gestalt", or overall, impression of the ad should mentally affront the reader and leave him with a sense of incompleteness or anxiety. This unsettled feeling of anxiety is resolved by ordering the product. When a product, a book for example, can be sold directly by sending in a coupon and around $10, this principle can be taken to extremes by using a "blind" or "mystery" ad. A blind ad takes subjective advertising to the limit by NOT REVEALING the contents of the book. The ad deliberately makes the reader guess at the contents. Curiosity, coupled with a solid guarantee, provide more than enough sales motivation when the selling price is $15 or less. Beyond that point, the cost of satisfying curiosity is simply too great.

Following are two ads for the book *Go For It*. The first illustrates an objective approach with strong emotional sales appeal. The second is a blind ad. Nowhere is the topic of the book revealed. Sales appeal is based on what the book can do for the reader, as well as building an overwhelming curiosity. In this case, the blind ad was the more successful of the two.

When writing an ad, keep statements simple and short. Do not confuse the reader with longwinded explanations. Paragraphs should be concise and to the point. They must carry the greatest possible **wallop** per word. Each paragraph must make its point

# $1000
## A WEEK IS THE MINIMUM YOU WILL BE EARNING AS A PRECIOUS METALS DEALER

David Davies, Author

### IF YOU FOLLOW MY
### STEP BY STEP BUSINESS PLAN!

Several years ago, when gold was selling for less than $300. an ounce I was offered a heavy, 14k gold pocket watch in non-working condition by a fellow, we'll call him Joe, who owed me money but didn't have any. Neither of us knew much about pocket watches or gold but together we figured the old watch should be worth about $85 if it was in working condition. Well, Joe owed me $50. so we figured it for a good deal all around.

#### Hopes Dashed!

At the time, I was flat broke and unemployed having just been laid off. So I was pretty eager to turn my 'new' pocket watch into cash.

Now I'm a pretty methodical guy and I needed money badly. But, I didn't rush out to the first pawnshop and cash in the watch, no sir. I took it to a specialist in pocket watches listed in the phone book. He looked over my watch, grunted and groaned and finally said, "Can't be repaired." All my hopes were dashed!

#### The Best Deal of a Lifetime, I thought!

Then I remembered the 14k gold case. Maybe that had $50 worth of gold in it. So I phoned five different refiners and purchasers of precious metals.

They wanted to know the weight and the karat of the case. A friendly neighborhood jeweler weighed the case for me. Now, all that was left for me to do was call around and find who would pay the highest price for the small amount of gold I had.

This is what I had: 44 pennyweights of 14k gold; the best price I could get was $6.75 for each pennyweight.

## $297.00

$297.00 is what they paid me for my '$50' watch. I figured I'd made the best deal of my life!

#### Wasn't A Fluke

Now I know differently. That deal was lucky since it got me into the gold business but it wasn't a FLUKE. I've found techniques to buy that much gold and more everyday for a tenth to a half of its value. I've found sources of scrap gold you wouldn't believe existed!

#### Few Know Where the Gold Is Those Who Know Won't Tell!!

Today, with what I've learned AND with the increasing value of gold that same watch would bring me $457.74 or $407.74 profit on just ONE purchase. I make dozens of gold and silver purchases everyday. Not all of them bring in $400 profit but if YOU are not making $1000.00 a week as a precious metals dealer you have not read my revealing and explicit manual,

#### Go For It!

Go For It! will teach you all the ins and outs of the precious metals business including:
* History of gold and silver uses, why it is so valuable

* Testing for gold, silver, diamonds
* 5 little known sources for buying scrap gold that guarantee you a good income
* How to get started with little or NO cash
* 3 different business set-ups you can use
* SILVER Why now is the time to get started dealing and stockpiling silver for your own account
* Refineries — How to sell your gold for absolute top dollar
* Pitfalls to avoid and how to avoid them
* Appraising jewelry, jewelers markups
* Coins — how to purchase them low, sell them high
* Class Rings — why these are your biggest single profit makers
* BONUS SECTION—DIAMONDS
* The one absolute, foolproof test for the genuine diamond
* All you need to know about grading and appraising diamonds
* Current wholesale diamond prices
* Why you should ALWAYS purchase below wholesale unless you want to lose money
* How to buy diamond rings for $15 and resell for $150

FINALLY
* Why now is the ideal time to become a precious metals-diamond dealer.

#### If You Wait It Might Be Too Late. Don't Be Fooled!

There is a lot to learn. I learned the hard, expensive way, by trial and ERROR. You MUST benefit by my three years experience and by my revolutionary, proven successful techniques or your MONEY BACK!

Go For It! costs just $12.00, two dollars of which pays for FIRST CLASS postage and handling. I'm willing to practically give away my secret, proven techniques of gold, silver and diamond dealing because I NEED dealers. You see, my plan has been so successful for me that I've become a refiner of gold and it is to my advantage to have my volume to compete with the big outfits. It is my sincere hope that you will take advantage of my offer of training in Go For It! AND that you then sell your gold to my firm, Timberlake Precious Metals.

I intend for you to succeed in the gold business. And you must succeed, for your success is my success.

#### Don't Get Me Wrong!

I'm not asking for any favors and YOU will have to work hard and follow my plan to achieve the degree of success I have achieved. There are many refineries but I feel if I can help you to become a successful gold dealer AND offer you prompt service and top rates you will choose to deal with Timberlake Precious Metals until perhaps, you've

grown large enough to start your own refinery.

Gold is at a transitional low, but the experts say it is practically inevitable for the price of gold and silver to soar in the near future.

NOW IS the time to GO FOR IT, to become an established, highly solvent dealer so that you don't miss out on the fortunes to be made in the next bull market.

This is one of the few businesses you can start without a lot of capital, without a big investment in equipment or in years of training. There is no physical work involved and five hours a day devoted to the business is more than enough to make you well off.

ORDER Go For It! right now for $12.00 and I'll make you a charter member of Timberlake Precious Metals Dealer network!:
* The entire cost of the book will be refunded to you when you send in your first gold shipment.
* Charter members will have ONE year free consultation privileges on any and all aspects of the gold business.
* After your first gold shipment TPM will send you a certificate in your name proclaiming you a TRAINED PROFESSIONAL precious metals dealer authorized to deal with Timberlake Precious Metals. Your handsome certificate is suitable for framing.

#### IF YOU TRULY WANT TO WORK FOR YOURSELF
*Set your own hours and vacations*
*Make an unlimited income starting at $1000 a week*
*Be secure in a depression proof business of your own*
*This is the opportunity you've been searching for.*
**I GUARANTEE IT**
**ACT NOW!**

Sincerely,

*Davi H. Dar*

#### ORDER FORM

*Dave, if Go For It! is everything you say it is, I can start making big money soon after studying it AND I have nothing to lose.*

*So here's my $10 plus $2 for special rush shipment via first class mail. I understand that if I am not satisfied I can return the manual within 30 days for a prompt refund.*

☐ *CASH your manual shipped via 1st class mail within 48 hours of receipt of your order.*

☐ *CHECK*

☐ *MONEY ORDER*

☐ *GOLD. TPM will send you a check, the manual is FREE!*

and lead the reader irresistibly onward to the next. Follow these eleven steps when constructing a blind ad:

1. Headline: Grab the attention of the reader, and stop him cold!
2. Subheading: Clarify and amplify the headline, and lead the reader into the body of the ad.
3. First paragraph: Tantalize the reader.
4. Assure the reader that he can benefit without hard work or great expense. Show him that anyone can benefit.
5. Tell him what the book is NOT.
6. Relate personal information. Tell the reader a story about the genesis of the book and how it has helped you or those around you. Use about half the ad, if necessary, to get the story across.
7. If you have testimonials, use them here.
8. Build credibility. Give references, and explain why you would sell such a great plan for only $10. Inspire confidence.
9. Inspire the reader to take action. Ask for his order, then emphasize the dangers of delay. "In a month, you could be just 30 days older or well on your way to a fortune — you decide," or words to that effect.
10. Summarize all the benefits the reader gets by ordering.
11. Guarantee. A 30 day money-back guarantee is standard. Some go with 10 days, others a full year. Many advertisers are asking for POST-DATED checks. This policy builds consumer confidence and brings in more orders.

One advertiser offers a $20 cashiers check plus

your money back just for trying his plan. Unfortunately, there is NO WAY an average person could implement his plan, find out if it works, and return it in 30 days! This hurts other advertisers who don't resort to misleading gimmicks, and eventually hurts the entire mail-order industry, as the public becomes cynical and mail-shy.

At any rate, ALWAYS include an order coupon, whether in a space ad or in a direct mail piece. Keep it clear and simple, and include a detachable GUARANTEE. Keep in mind that the detached order coupon must fit within the BRE (business return envelope). We simplify matters for our customers by putting the mailing label right on the order coupon and sending it out in a #10 window envelope. The customer doesn't even have to fill in his name and address. He merely checks the appropriate box, fills in his credit card number and expiration date, if required, and places the order coupon into the BRE. Since our mailing lists are ordered with the key code right on the labels, each order comes to us with the order key right on it. This technique also avoids the difficulties encountered in trying to decipher a customer's illegible handwriting.

Other effective and legitimate techniques to increase response are:

1. Don't ask for immediate payment. Send a bill.
2. Use 2 colors in the sales letter.
3. Include a full street address — never just a P.O. box.
4. Include a toll-free or regular business telephone number for credit card orders. Do not use your home telephone number. People tend to order on impulse, often at 2 AM your time!
5. Offer a FREE bonus for prompt response.

This can be a free mystery gift, an extra report or personal consultation privileges.

6.  Assure PROMPT DELIVERY.

If you bill your customers, ALWAYS send a terrific bounceback offer along with the bill. In fact, whenever you communicate with a customer, include a bounceback offer as well. At TPM Publishing, even REFUNDS are sent out with a bounceback offer enclosed.

When a customer receives a bill and a NEW offer, he knows that he must pay the first bill in order to get the second offer. He is more likely to pay promptly because he is eager to have the latest product rushed to him.

## Elements of an Objective Ad

1.  **Stop** the reader cold in his tracks.
2.  Build a mounting **interest** in the product.
3.  Turn mere interest into a burning **desire** to have the product.
4.  **Convince** the reader with testimonials, references, and proof.
5.  Call for immediate **action**, ordering the product now.

Never tell all! Follow the above formula, but, whatever you do, never tell all. Build interest and excitement by leaving just enough unsaid to tantalize the reader's imagination. One ad I read sold information on how to buy gold and silver scrap. It was so detailed that I skipped ordering the book and immediately began buying gold. The ad sold me on the idea of the business itself, but NOT on the benefits of buying the book.

## Focus the Ad on Basic Human Emotions, as Many as Possible, to Sell the Product

## as Many as Possible, to Sell the Product

Were you, for example, to focus solely on the emotion "avarice" or greed, your ad would neglect those with charitable emotions, those for whom SECURITY is important, those who crave idleness, and many, many others. Outline all the emotions. Choose the one most likely to sell your product, and then weave a matrix of all the other emotional appeals possible around your main theme.

## Answer Natural Objections Before the Reader Perceives Them

All products must be evaluated because there are usually valid objections to buying almost anything. No potential customer wants to be force-fed a product. The reader must be led, inevitably, to his own conclusion that he must have the product. Ad copy should be personal, as though written from one friend to another. It should provide the data necessary for the customer to overcome potential objectives, thus leading to his decision to purchase. Lead the customer — don't coerce him! This does not mean that an ad can't be BOLD. Your ad should express confidence. Don't plead for an order; simply ask for it. I especially like Chrysler Corporation's parting shot on its televised ads with Lee Iococca: "If you can find a better built car, buy it!".

Do you need a professional copywriter? Assuming that you have a reasonably saleable product, the ONLY THING THAT STANDS BETWEEN YOU AND SUCCESS IS WORDS ON PAPER! A simple thought, yes, but the transition from thought to paper is critical.

Copywriting is both an art and a science. Just changing a headline can result in one percent more response. When a million ads are mailed, this simple change can result in 10,000 additional orders. At $19.95 each, that's a $200,000 headline! If the difference between the copy of a professional versus an amateur copywriter came down to JUST the headline, it could be worth almost $200,000 to have a professional prepare the copy. Over the life of the ad (generally a year or more), this could amount to a million dollars in greater revenue. Notice that I said **could**, not **does**. No professional copywriter guarantees his work. **He uses** known mail-order principles for maximizing **response**. He has, or should have, the knack for boiling down a product's selling appeal into a thick, zesty broth that will attract hungry consumers.

A gifted amateur, on the other hand, may hit on a technique overlooked by professionals as too amateurish or outlandish. He may have more genuine enthusiasm for the product. If this comes through in his ad copy, he will sell more than the professional. Testing and refining are the great equalizers. A mediocre amateur copywriter can test and refine his ads until he has a winner that will pull in as much response as the best copy to be found anywhere.

My first two ads were a blind, or mystery, ad and an objective sales ad. I had no idea which would be better, so I mailed half to one list and half to another. For example, I tested two different lists of 5,000 names each. I mailed 2,500 mystery and 2,500 objective ads to each list. The response was 3% for the objective ad and 6.4% for the mystery ad from the stronger of the two lists. For my next mailing, I naturally discarded the objective ad and the weaker mailing list. Later refining brought as much as a 9.2% response to the blind ad. When mailing to rented mailing lists, 4% is considered an average and 5% an excellent response.

Whether you employ a professional copywriter or choose to write your own ads comes down to a personal value judgement. If you have the funds available, you probably should do both and test your copy against that of the professional. Remember, once a professional has designed an ad for you, it is yours to use as much as you want in order to make as much money as you can. If his ad is hot, you may spend $1,500 to reap a fortune. Also, you could prepare two of your own ads for testing purposes and have BOTH of them FAIL. You can be sure that the test will set you back $1,500 and might even discourage you from trying again. On the other hand, amateurs have become top-flight copywriters through study, instinct, and persistent testing.

## The Five Selling Media

There are five direct marketing media for selling information-related products. These are listed as follows. We are most interested in the first three.

1. Classified advertising in magazines and newspapers
2. Display advertising in magazines and newspapers
3. Direct mail solicitation
4. Telephone solicitation
5. Spot 1 or 2 minute television ads

*Classified Advertising*

Placing unillustrated, brief, 30 word or less advertisements in magazines and newspapers is the way to get started in the mail-order business with the lowest initial expense. However, the cost per order is greater than for either display advertising or direct mail solicitation.

*Display or Full Page Space Advertising*

This costs more than classified advertising and is simpler than direct mail solicitation. When used properly, it can generate a tremendous number of orders and a large customer list.

*Direct Mail Solicitation*

This is the technique of the pros. With increased postage costs and the high cost of renting mailing lists, the initial expense can be great. However, volume orders and reorders from established customers make this the mainstay of the business.

*Telephone Sales*

Boiler room, high pressure salespeople telephone hundreds of customers daily, with a high conversion rate from inquiries to sales. This technique is in its infancy. It is already being used by investment houses and for record and magazine sales, etc.

*Short Television Ads*

Television is most effective in regional marketing during non-prime time. It works best for products requiring a visual demonstration. It is effective in selling products purchased on impulse, especially if a toll-free number is provided. With the right product, television ads can sell hundreds of thousands of items in a short time. For example, GINZU KNIVES sold 300,000 sets at $19.95 each in just one month!

## Classified Advertising Techniques

Your ad is designed to get the reader to request FREE additional information, using the fewest possible words. Never ask for money directly in the ad. Use a two step approach. The reader is intrigued enough to request free information from you. You immediately respond with a mailing package consisting of a four page sales letter, a brochure (if illustrations are needed), and an order coupon with BRE.

You can make more money more quickly using direct mail solicitation by first purchasing the names of potential customers from a list broker. Most brokers won't rent fewer than 5,000 names from each list. At the present cost of $60 to $65 per thousand names, this is a significant extra initial expense over the cost of a classified ad. Compared with a 5% response from a direct mailing, getting an equal number of orders from classified advertising would require 1667 inquiries and a 15% conversion rate. The conversion rate is calculated by dividing the number of orders by the number of inquiries.

As an example, were you to choose a mailing list (just make an educated guess, since you cannot afford to test several) and mail out the minimum 5,000 letters, you might get 5% response, or 250 orders. We will calculate and compare the advertising costs to obtain these 250 orders using direct mail solicitation and classified advertising.

*Direct Mail Expenses for Advertising*

| | | |
|---|---|---|
| Cost of renting mailing list | | |
| (5,000 @ $65/1,000) | = $ | 325 |
| Cost of printing sales letter | | |
| (5,000 @ .07) | = $ | 350 |
| Cost of mailing service | | |
| (5,000 @ $19/1,000) | = $ | 95 |
| Cost of postage | | |
| (5,000 @ .11, bulk rate) | = $ | 550 |
| Total direct mail advertising cost | = $ | 1,320 |

The average classified ad runs 25 words at $4 per

word. Thus, each ad would cost $100. Each ad is projected to generate 134 inquiries over a two month period. If you have a 15% conversion rate, you will net 20 orders from the 134 inquiries. To get 250 orders, you must place 12 or 13 ads, at $100 each. A breakdown of the advertising expenses using classified advertising follows:

*Classified Ad Expenses for Advertising*

| | | |
|---|---|---|
| Cost of placing classified ads | | |
| (13 @ $100) | = | $ 1,300 |
| Cost of sales letters | | |
| (1,742 @ .07) | = | $    122 |
| Cost of mailing sales letters | | |
| (1,742 @ .20) | = | $    348.40 |
| Total Classified Ad Expense | = | $ 1,770.40 |

To round out the picture, let us complete the calculation of total sales, other expenses, and profit using the two sales techniques. Both total sales and other expenses must be the same for 250 orders, no matter how they were generated.

*Total Sales*

| | | |
|---|---|---|
| 250 books @ $14.95 | = | $ 3,737.50 |

*Other Expenses*

| | | |
|---|---|---|
| Cost of books and shipping | | |
| (250 @ $2) | = | $    500 |

Your profit is the difference between the total sales and the total expenses (the sum of advertising costs plus other expenses). Your profit using direct mailing is $1,937.50, while your profit using classified advertising is only $1,367.50 — a difference of $550 on only 250 orders!

## Keeping Records

It is extremely important to keep accurate records in a mail-order business. It is only through your record-keeping that you can determine which ad is the most powerful, which advertising lead is the most enticing, and how well your product is selling. Good records are the followup of good testing.

Keep copies of all ads and mailing material in a loose-leaf binder or scrapbook. You may also want to include a record of all the keys you have used, either in that book or in a separate folder. The separate sheets of records per key or publication will enable you to determine which ads are bringing in the most profits.

You can make your own record sheet with a pen and ruler or you can photocopy the example on the next page. At the top of the sheet, place the name of the publication in which the ad appeared, the issue number and/or date, the date the issue was placed on sale, the address key, the size and cost of the ad, which ad you used, the price of the product, and the profit (which you will calculate later).

The main body of the record sheet has two main categories: inquiries and sales. First, the number of days should be listed in a column at the left. These do not coincide with the days of the month. Instead, start with the first day that responses come in. The subheadings under "Inquiries" should be: Date Received, Number Received, and Running Total. The subheadings under "Orders" should be "Number of Orders Received, Running Total of Orders, Cash Sales, and Running Total of Cash Sales. These record sheets will help you to determine the responses to classified ads,

# RECORD SHEET

PUBLICATION _____ ISSUE_____ ON SALE _____

KEY_____ SIZE OF ADV_____ COST OF ADV_____

PRODUCT ADV._____ SELLING PRICE_____ PROFIT_____

REMARKS _____

| No of Days | INQUIRIES | | | SALES | | | | No of Days | INQUIRIES | | | SALES | | | |
|---|---|---|---|---|---|---|---|---|---|---|---|---|---|---|---|
| | Date Rec'd | No Rec'd | Running Total | Daily No of Orders | Total No. of Orders | Daily Cash Sales | Total Cash Sales | | Date Rec'd | No Rec'd | Running Total | Daily No of Orders | Total No. of Orders | Daily Cash Sales | Total Cash Sales |
| 1 | | | | | | | | 42 | | | | | | | |
| 2 | | | | | | | | 43 | | | | | | | |
| 3 | | | | | | | | 44 | | | | | | | |
| 4 | | | | | | | | 45 | | | | | | | |
| 5 | | | | | | | | 46 | | | | | | | |
| 6 | | | | | | | | 47 | | | | | | | |
| 7 | | | | | | | | 48 | | | | | | | |
| 8 | | | | | | | | 49 | | | | | | | |
| 9 | | | | | | | | 50 | | | | | | | |
| 10 | | | | | | | | 51 | | | | | | | |
| 11 | | | | | | | | 52 | | | | | | | |
| 12 | | | | | | | | 53 | | | | | | | |
| 13 | | | | | | | | 54 | | | | | | | |
| 14 | | | | | | | | 55 | | | | | | | |
| 15 | | | | | | | | 56 | | | | | | | |
| 16 | | | | | | | | 57 | | | | | | | |
| 17 | | | | | | | | 58 | | | | | | | |
| 18 | | | | | | | | 59 | | | | | | | |
| 19 | | | | | | | | 60 | | | | | | | |
| 20 | | | | | | | | 61 | | | | | | | |
| 21 | | | | | | | | 62 | | | | | | | |
| 22 | | | | | | | | 63 | | | | | | | |
| 23 | | | | | | | | 64 | | | | | | | |
| 24 | | | | | | | | 65 | | | | | | | |
| 25 | | | | | | | | 66 | | | | | | | |
| 26 | | | | | | | | 67 | | | | | | | |
| 27 | | | | | | | | 68 | | | | | | | |
| 28 | | | | | | | | 69 | | | | | | | |
| 29 | | | | | | | | 70 | | | | | | | |
| 30 | | | | | | | | 71 | | | | | | | |
| 31 | | | | | | | | 72 | | | | | | | |
| 32 | | | | | | | | 73 | | | | | | | |
| 33 | | | | | | | | 74 | | | | | | | |
| 34 | | | | | | | | 75 | | | | | | | |
| 35 | | | | | | | | | | | | | | | |
| 36 | | | | | | | | | | | | | | | |
| 37 | | | | | | | | | | | | | | | |
| 38 | | | | | | | | | | | | | | | |
| 39 | | | | | | | | | | | | | | | |
| 40 | | | | | | | | | | | | | | | |
| 41 | | | | | | | | | | | | | | | |

orders from sales literature, and how much money you are making.

To calculate the cost per inquiry, divide the cost of the ad by the total number of inquiries received. To find the cost of advertising per order, add the total cost of mailing the sales packet to the cost of the ad, and divide by the number of orders received. In the above example, the advertising cost per order using classified advertising is $7.56, assuming a conversion rate of 15%. It is just $5.28 per order using direct mail solicitation, assuming a 5% response.

Classified advertising allows the beginner to get started in the mail-order field gradually and safely, albeit at a greater cost per order obtained. Also, the orders generated from classified advertising trickle in over an extended period. The same 250 orders probably took three to four months to acquire using classified. Three weeks after a direct mailing, 80% of your orders are in, and you don't have to wait for magazine publication schedules.

I started my business using direct mailing from the outset. If the price per book is $14.95, the break-even point is a response rate of between 2% and 2.3%. This is low enough so that I consider the risk to be worthwhile. In addition, it is physically impossible to generate a really large income relying solely on classified advertising because there simply aren't enough of the right kind of publications in which to advertise. The process is cumbersome at best.

## Direct Mailing Solicitation Techniques

If you sincerely want to make a SUBSTANTIAL INCOME, I recommend starting out with direct mailing from the very beginning. Start with adequate capital, as I recommended in Chapter 3. If you count yourself as a former "failure" in the direct mailing field, it is probably because you dabbled, rather than plunged in. Doing something halfway is worse than not doing it at all! It is like learning to ride a horse side-saddle — ONLY HALFWAY MOUNTED! The ride is more precarious, and you are more likely to fall off than the rider with both feet mounted securely in the stirrups. Take pains to do it right the first time, and you will be better off.

## Mailing

You can obtain a bulk rate permit from the post office if you send out at least 200 identical pieces at a time. The pieces must be pre-sorted for destination in exact zip code sequence. The bulk rate cost is lower, but it takes much longer for the mail to be delivered.

The most important aspect to mailing your sales literature is the quality of the list of people to whom you are sending it. A brilliant sales piece won't work if it is not sent to the right people. That is why you need to test which category list to use and then which particular list within the category.

Your own mailing list is the best one because you know to what these people have already responded since you, yourself, have keyed the responses. You have already profiled the potential buyer; you have already written a sales piece aimed at that buyer; and you will definitely make money from that buyer.

Although you can buy or rent lists of names and addresses from list brokers, you can never be sure how well the list will respond to your sales package. Test different headings, prices, and layouts.

All mail-order business involves testing and retesting. Once you have found a successful advertisement, stick with it, and reap the profits. Every time you rent a new list, you MUST FIRST test a small portion of it to determine whether mailing to the entire list would be profitable. By combining a mailing to one or several already tested lists with a mailing to small portions of new, untested lists, you can test safely and reap big profits simultaneously.

On a mailing of 100,000, I mail to 80 or 85 thousand names from lists already tested. I am thus assured that at least 80 or 85% of my mailing will generate a satisfactory response. That leaves 15,000 names. Taking just 5,000 names from each one allows me to test three new lists. Preferably, these three new lists will have a total of 85,000 more names available. That way, you have enough names for your next mailing.

If your 100,000 mailing is successful with one product, it is possible to remail to the SAME 100,000 names using a different, but related, product. The response should not be significantly different, assuming, of course, that the advertising for the second product is equally effective. Even mailing the *original* ad to the same 100,000 names two weeks later can bring in as many as 60% of the orders originally obtained.

**For long-term success in mail-order, you must have a good bounceback offer.**

Single product successes are rare. Do not sell just one book on a subject. Follow up with an offer of a related book or product. A book on muscle building can be followed with offers of exercise equipment. A book on gold dealing can be followed up with offers of gold dealers' equipment and related books. A book on diet can sell and CONTINUE TO SELL diet supplements. Reorders of this consumable product provide the seller with a continuous source of income WITH-

OUT THE EXPENSE OF SECURING NEW NAMES. This is the ideal. It is what you should aim for.

Note that the original book can be the bearer of the advertising. The cost of printing several pages devoted to advertising is minimal. If you sell 20,000 books, you have 20,000 **Long Term** advertisements out there. Orders can come in months and even years after the book was first sold. Always include an order blank, right in the pages of the book. Also, always include a separate advertising flyer with every product sent out.

Let us say that you have sold a book on diet. From an ad in the back of the book, you receive an order for iron tablets. When you ship the tablets, include a catalogue of all your other dietary supplements.

How do you find diet supplements to sell retail? Write to the manufacturer directly. Order a copy of the New York City yellow pages, and look up several manufacturers. Virtually any product imaginable can be found in a Directory of Manufacturers at the library. You can even order a list of several thousand names and addresses of manufacturers and distributors of any product you choose through a large mailing list broker such as:

Edith Roman Assoc., Inc.
875 Avenue of the Americas
New York, NY 10001
1-800-223-2194

Check as well with other brokers listed at the end of the chapter.

When you write to a manufacturer, mention that you will be selling quantities of his product through mail-order and tell him that you require a complete product description, any "in-house" advertising that he may have, and a confidential dealers' wholesale price list with suggested retail prices. When your business grows really big, you may be able to have your own label on the merchandise you purchase for resale.

## Mechanics of Direct Mail Solicitation

Step. 1   Prepare a mailing package
    a. Write it yourself or have a professional do it.
    b. Have it illustrated and typeset by a professional.
    c. Contract with an offset printer to print your mailing piece: #10 outside envelope, 4 page sales letter, brochure (if necessary), order coupon with attached guarantee, and BRE. Pay no more than 7¢ each.

Step. 2   Contact a list broker.
Decide which lists to test and how many names to whom you can afford to mail. Give the broker a key code to distinguish each list. For instance, if you order 5,000 of Robert Schindler's 1983 buyers names, you could code the order RS3. If you test 2 different sales letters, use 2 differently colored order coupons. Now go ahead and order the names.

Step. 3   Contract with a mailing service to stuff, label, stamp, and send out your mailing. This service is well worth it. I once stuffed, sealed, addressed, and stamped 1,000 envelopes, and it darned near drove me crazy!

Step. 4   Be sure you have sufficient inventory on hand to fill your highest projected response. A good response is 5%. If you are mailing to 10,000 names, 500 people may order your book. Have 500 **In Hand Before** doing the mailing! The law states that all orders must be sent within 30 days of receipt, or you must offer to return the money. One mistake like this could wipe out your new business!

Step 5.    Fill all orders on the same day received or by the next day. Your first orders will start to trickle in ten days or so after the mailing. Two weeks after the mailing date, you will have received approximately 30% of the total number of orders you will eventually get. Multiply by three to get an approximate total figure. If this projected total is close to or over 5% of your mailing, you have a winning combination.

Step. 6    Deposit your money in the bank, and *immediately* order more names, books, and mailing packages. Spend *all* the income on this next, larger mailing.

## Testing

We mentioned key coding orders in Step 2. You will not succeed in mail-order without testing. Testing implies that you are able to measure the results of each mailing list, each different brochure, and, in space advertising, each ad in the various magazines you have used. This means that whenever you place an advertisement, whether classified or display, you need to code the address so that you know which ad generated the inquiry.

This coding system is called "keying the address". Take a look at those ads you have been studying. See those codes? Department WD-5, Division 9A, Drawer 4B, etc. These are all address keys to use in recording and tabulating responses. They are most important in testing the pull of your ads. You can use any combination of letters and numbers to code the address. Most businesses use the words department, suite number, room number, division, or drawer. A simple key is the intials of the name of the publication and number indicating the month of the issue. But you can use any code that you can easily remember and manage.

Always test just one factor at a time. If you think that another color of paper might improve your response, test that factor alone. Mail the original color brochure to half your list and the new color to the remaining half. Have your list broker choose a *random selection* of half the names by requesting an $n^{th}$ *name selection*. Were you to order 5,000 names, your broker would make a computer $n^{th}$ name selection of 2,500 names. He would do a second $n^{th}$ name selection of 2,500 names on the remaining names in the entire list.

Lists are ordered in ZIP CODE sequence in order to qualify for bulk rate postage, currently 11¢ a letter. A broker could possibly fill your order from the low numbered zip codes in New England. The second 2,500 names could have zip codes from the West Coast. This throws a joker into your testing because of differences in climate and attitudes. An ad for a wood stove might get a good response in New England and "bomb" in California. The fact that Californians don't order many wood stoves is interesting, but it doesn't help you to distinguish which is the more effective brochure.

To tell which order came from which color brochure, simply use a different color for each order coupon. If you receive 253 blue order coupons out of 5,000 blue brochures mailed, then 5.1% have responded. If only 179 out of 5,000 responded to your red brochure by sending back their red coupon, then you can tell that this color generated a 3.6% response. Next time, mail all blue brochures.

In this case, the results of your testing are obvious. A 5.1% response is clearly better than a 3.6% response, and the results of the test told you exactly what to do. But what do you do if the difference is .2% or .3% instead of 1.5%? Is it not possible that such a small difference could be due to chance or random factors? If this small difference is due to chance, and you assume that it is not, then you will either throw out perfectly good advertising copy or go to the expense of having new brochures printed. You have a nagging worry, "Am I doing the right thing? Are the results of the test definitive?"

Application of statistical techniques comes to your rescue here. You do not need to know or evaluate the formulae involved. We have done that for you. All that you need to do is to make sure that you test each factor separately on a total of at least 3,000 names by sending each brochure to at least 1,500 names. The number receiving each brochure should be equal. If you do that and get a difference of .2% or more, statistics says that you can be 99% sure that the brochure, list, etc., from which you obtained the higher response is, indeed, better, *all other factors being equal.*

If you are testing two different lists and get a difference of .2%, you might well decide that it will be profitable to mail to the statistically weaker list, even though you know that the weaker list is not quite as good as the stronger. If your difference is as little as .2% or .3%, other unknown factors might come into play that would invalidate the statistical analysis.

## Ordering the Right List

The best list is one that

1.) includes people who have ordered a product

similar to yours in the same price range, and
2.) has all fresh names, that is, people who have made their purchase in the last 90 days.

Just as mystery story addicts read every mystery they can obtain, **Opportunity Seekers** place repeated orders for new opportunities. At least 5% of them will order a professionally presented new business opportunity at any given time. It is estimated that the opportunity seeker market consists of over 50 million people.

An empathetic broker with the right lists can help you make hundreds of thousands of dollars! **Warning:** Never economize on mailing lists. Some mailing list companies promote cheap lists for as little as $15 per thousand in huge quantities. Do not buy them because they will cost you money every time. Expect to pay $60 to $65 per thousand names for fresh up-to-date lists that have recently been "cleaned". A "clean" list has had duplicate names and undeliverable addresses removed. Cheap lists may be derived from telephone books for all we know. The people on them may hate mail-order. The list might be four years old. During that time, people on them could have moved, died, or just simply lost interest in whatever the original offer was.

## Use Credit to Pyramid Profits

I strongly recommend using some of your seed capital to do your initial tests. For only about $2,500, you can test 2 lists of 5,000 each and 2 or more brochures. This figure does not include the cost of purchasing the 500 or so products needed for inventory. This expense will, of course, vary, depending on the product.

Expect to just break even on your initial test. If you can rent 1,500 to 2,000 names from each list, then do a smaller initial mailing, perhaps to three lists of 2,000 each, for a total of 6,000. All you want at this point is test results telling you which list(s) and/or mailing package(s) are effective.

Analyse the results. Divide the orders received from each different combination of list and brochure by the total number mailed to that combination. If any particular combination of list and brochure resulted in a 5% or greater rate of orders, you have a winning combination that you can use. If no combination comes close to that figure, go back to the drawing board. Either your lists are poor or your mailing package lacks sales punch. If all three mailing lists you tested were highly recommended and still yielded a poor response, you probably have to redo your sales letter.

Spice up the sales letter with 2 colors (black ink, with blue headline, for example). Use handwritten messages written in blue ink in the margins and the post script. A picture of yourself often adds credibility. A P.S. offering a "freebee" helps. The price of your product could be a factor. Is the price high enough to scare people off? On the other hand, if it is too low, people will unconsciously think that your product is worthless. You may actually sell more at a higher price. A friend wrote a book on how to build a log cabin. He sold 400 copies at $2 each. He would have done much better if he had sold only 250 copies at $10 each. Last, but not least, check your ad copy. Read it through as though you had never seen it before. Do you get all excited? If not, change it so that it does excite you. In the final analysis, only testing and more testing will help you determine what to do. The money spent on testing will come back later manyfold in the form of increased profits.

Now that you have found a combination that works, plan your next mailing. You can usually get thirty to ninety days credit from printers and the mailing service. The U.S. Postal Service and many list brokers require UP FRONT payment for postage and names. If you can persuade the list broker to advance his names on thirty days credit, do it.

Then, on a mailing to 25,000 names, your up front postage cost is $2,750 ($.11 per letter). This is about what your entire test mailing has cost you. If you can't get credit from the list broker, you must find another $1,650 from your reserves.

Let us examine the sales, expenses, and profit picture resulting from this initial mailing. We will also examine your total available cash after the mailing is completed. Assume that you mail to 25,000 names and that the response rate is 5%. We will also assume that each product costs $2 to produce, $1 to ship, and that it sells for $14.95.

*Sales*

| | | |
|---|---|---|
| 1,250 @ $14.95 | = | $ 18,687.50 |

*Expenses*

| | | |
|---|---|---|
| Cost of postage (25,000 @ .11) | = | $ 2,750 (prepaid) |
| Cost of mailing list rental (25,000 @ $65/1,000) | = | $ 1,625 (prepaid) |
| Cost of brochures (25,000 @ .07) | = | $ 1,750 |
| Cost of mailing service (25,000 @ $19/1,000) | = | $ 475 |
| Cost of products (1,250 @ $2) | = | $ 2,500 |
| Cost of shipping products (1,250 @ $1) | = | $ 1,250 |
| Total expenses | = | $ 10,350 |

*Profit*

| | | |
|---|---|---|
| Sales | = | $ 18,687.50 |
| Expenses | = | $ 10,350.00 |
| Profit | = | $ 8,337.50 |

*Cash on Hand*

| | | |
|---|---|---|
| Profit | = | $ 8,337.50 |
| Prepaid expenses recovered | = | $ 4,375.00 |
| Total cash on hand | = | $ 12,712.50 |

You should have over $12,000 in your pocket within 6 weeks of your mailing! This may be the most money you have ever seen at one time. Do not spend it — not one penny!

Within two weeks of the date of the mailing, you should know whether the mailing will pay off. About 30% of your orders are in. Just multiply by 3.3 to project the total number of orders you will eventually receive. Why? Because as soon as you know that your first mailing has been successful, you can order names for a second, larger mailing! In fact, you can just about triple the size of your next mailing, provided that you have pretested large enough lists. **Important:** Each time you mail, test 5,000 names each from two or three new lists. If you test 5,000 names out of a total list of 25,000, you are left with 20,000 names to whom to mail the next time.

With $12,000 in available cash, you can now order and pay for 65,000 names. We can look at the sales, expenses, profit, and available cash after this second mailing, just as we did for the first, assuming the same 5% response and other expenses.

*Sales*

| | | |
|---|---|---|
| 3,250 @ $14.95 | = | $ 48,567.50 |

*Expenses*

| | | | | |
|---|---|---|---|---|
| Cost of postage | | | | |
| (65,000 @ .11) | = | $ | 7,150 | (prepaid) |
| Cost of mailing list rental | | | | |
| (65,000 @ $65/1,000) | = | $ | 4,225 | (prepaid) |
| Cost of mailing service | | | | |
| (65,000 @ $19/1,000) | = | $ | 1,235 | |
| Cost of brochures | | | | |
| (65,000 @ .07) | = | $ | 4,550 | |
| Cost of products | | | | |
| (3,250 @ $2) | = | $ | 6,500 | |
| Cost of shipping products | | | | |
| (3,250 @ $1) | = | $ | 3,250 | |
| Total expenses | = | $ | 26,910 | |

*Profit*

| | | | |
|---|---|---|---|
| Sales | = | $ | 48,567.50 |
| Expenses | = | $ | 26,910.00 |
| Profit | = | $ | 21,657.50 |

*Cash on hand*

| | | | |
|---|---|---|---|
| Profit | = | $ | 21,657.50 |
| Prepaid | | | |
| expenses recovered | = | $ | 11,375.00 |
| Total cash on hand | = | $ | 33,032.50 |

Your cash on hand has just increased to about $33,000 as a result of this second mailing. Your actual profit and cash on hand will probably be somewhat greater because you will begin to get volume discounts both on your product and on the cost of printing your sales literature. Printing costs for brochures can drop to as little as 3¢ each in larger quantities (over 50,000). Shop around. Product costs should also drop sharply as quantities increase. A book that costs

$2 to purchase in small quantities can be reordered in volume. Ten thousand books may well cost only $5,000, or 50¢ each.

You can continue to pyramid your mailings to ever increasing profits, as long as your supply of names holds out. Another option is to stabilize your mailings by mailing to 50,000 new prospects every six weeks. That allows you six or seven mailings a year. Never mail during December. It is the worst possible month for mail-order. June and July are also weak. Do yourself a favor and take the summer off. That leaves October, January, September, August, November, February, March, April, and May in order of likely response strength.

Mail every six weeks to 50,000 names at a time during the course of a year, and you will have total sales of almost a quarter of a million dollars! Follow up with a second book or other bounceback offer, and you will add forty to fifty thousand dollars to your gross income. At the end of a year, allow a list broker to rent out your 15,000 name customer list. List rental should give you another $10,000 to $15,000. The broker keeps 20% of this for his services, so you pocket a $12,000 windfall.

If you couple direct mailings with space advertising, an annual sales volume approaching a **Half Million Dollars** is possible! The second and third years become even better as you develop new products and keep expanding and selling to your own customer list.

Your customer list costs you a considerable amount of money to develop over the years. It represents one of your most valuable assets. Your customers will eventually trust you and look forward eagerly to your new offerings. It is a fact borne out by statistics that the response from your own "in house" mailing list will be double or triple that obtained from an outside rented list. I know of one man who mailed to 300,000 of his own customers and received a whopping 17% response. That comes to 51,000 orders of his new product, all within 2 months! In case you are interested, this person sells vitamins and other nutritional products. His offer was to allow his own customers to market the products themselves through a *multilevel sales organization*. This concept has all the requirements mentioned in Chapter 3 for outrageous success.

Lesson #1 said that of the three ingredients to any sale, the marketing of the product is far more important than the product itself. Lesson #2 told us to sell something that results in multiple, continuous sales, yielding high profits for little effort.

Our friend obviously has his marketing down pat if he has 300,000 satisfied, repeat customers. Secondly, he is selling a product in one of the *can't miss* categories: "health and self improvement", "sex and romance", and "making lots of money". In fact, he has combined "health and nutrition" with "money making" — a winning combination.

Does this give you any ideas? Does it get you excited? If it doesn't, you have missed something along the way or you are not using your imagination.

Can you imagine the potential of 51,000 *distributors*, each selling to untold thousands more distributors, and so on, for five levels? Diet products and vitamins are a consumable product. That results in multiple, continuous sales, yielding high profits. Selling them is nearly effortless because established customers tend to order more product as it is consumed. With a multilevel sales organization, each distributor has several, even hundreds, of lower level distributors working for him. Sales can mount quickly to enormous figures. Those participating at the inception of the program have a good chance for becoming wealthy.

Now, hopefully, you·are beginning to see the kind of thinking, the kind of concepts necessary to success. You are developing a **Mind for Success**.

## Personal Challenge

Right now, start thinking of a promotion and a product that incorporate the success lessons #1 and #2 given above. Try to develop an idea just as potent as the true example just given.

Believe me, this kind of opportunity is available to *anyone!* But, you must start somewhere. The millionaire (I'm sure that he is a millionaire by now, since he started his plan last summer) who did this multi-level promotion paid his dues first. He became an expert mail-order advertiser — good enough to have 300,000 customers. He found and promoted an ideal product, diet supplements and vitamins. He did research on multilevel sales organizations, and came up with a winner. None of what he did was impossible, obviously, or even difficult at the time. It was a developmental process, leading from modest success to overwhelming, **outrageous success.** The kind of success that makes a person a millionaire in a month and a multimillionaire within a year does not come overnight. It is built step by step.

## Space Advertising

Full page display advertisements in magazines and newspapers are selling millions of books and other mail-order products each year. They are ideal for selling unusual products that are not available in stores. Space ads do well for products needing a picture or illustration to be fully appreciated. The goal, as far as you are concerned, is to get the public to order directly from the ad. For this reason, a detachable order coupon is a necessary part of any space ad. Response increases when the customer has an easy way to order.

Success is equivalent to gross sales of two to four times the cost of the ad. Unbelievably successful ads crop up now and then. An example is the ad for a money-making plan published in *The National Enquirer*. The ad cost $22,000, and resulted in $192,000 worth of orders in a short time! If you get gross sales of 3 to 5 times the cost of your ad, you should place the ad in all the appropriate publications.

You should then buy or lease a personal computer (we like the KAYPRO 10), a letter quality printer, a postage meter, and hire an adept secretary. Why bother with all this? Because, when you receive 200 to 1,000 orders a day, you will require these tools and personnel just to keep organized.

We lease a Pitney-Bowes postage meter. The amount of time it saves is amazing. There is a wide choice of computers available. Look for one that has a good list management program, the capacity to store *at least* 25,000 names and addresses, and the possibility for easy future expansion of storage capacity when it becomes necessary.

To have a shot at this kind of success, you need to do the following:

1. Prepare a professionally written full page ad.
2. Price your product so that gross (or total) sales will be at least 2 to 4 times the cost of the ad.
3. Analyse the type of prospect to whom

your product would appeal.

4. Select magazines most likely to be read by your prospects.

A professional will prepare your ad for anywhere from $1,000 to $4,000. You can also either adapt a full page ad from your mailing package or write your own ad from scratch. See opportunity ads in *Salesman's Opportunity* magazine and others listed at the end of this chapter. Don't copy their words — just imitate and *improve* on their technique.

If you use a copywriter, find one who specializes in mail-order advertising. Ask to see samples of his currently running ads — magazine ads using an order coupon. If possible, contact the advertiser himself to see just how successful the ads were. If you can communicate with the copywriter *and* you like his ads, hire him. Give him all your ideas, previous advertisements, and a sample of the product itself.

Agree on the end result of his work. You are buying his time and his inspiration. He must, therefore, be inspired in order to do his best work. If your copywriter lacks enthusiasm, the copy will be dull. Do everything in your power to make him enthusiastic about your product. If he cannot get himself fired up for your project, get someone else who can. Bargain for the final fee. You should only accept an ad on which you, yourself, are 100% sold. An agreement to that effect should be made at the outset. If you do not like his ad, and he cannot convince you how great it is, have him redo those sections which you feel are weak. Finally, after you have agreed on a price for his services, offer him a bonus, say $500 when the ad pays off (with gross sales at least three times the ad cost).

Some advertising agencies will do a test ad on credit if they think you have a blockbuster of a pro-

*An example of a successful opportunity ad.*

108

duct. They then take their fee off the top, as orders come in. Large agencies like to increase their advertising budget by a factor of 10 each time a test works out well. For example, they place a test ad in a publication, at a cost of $2,500. It results in gross sales of $8,100. They then spend $25,000 on more ads in similar publications. Another criterion of success often employed for a space ad is that an ad must yield a profit of 100% of its cost. As we have already seen, profit is calculated by deducting all your expenses, including the cost of the ad and making and shipping your product, from the total (gross) sales. If the ad meets this test, it is considered successful.

Hiring the best professional copywriter you can get may be the most profitable move you can make. Once a copywriter has written a successful ad, you literally have a hold on the goose that lays the golden eggs. With the right product, you may still be making money from that same ad years later. You may decide to have him prepare a whole series of money-making ads for you.

Hiring the best mail-order advertising agency may *save* you a small fortune. Sure, you can save the 15% commission by establishing your own IN-HOUSE AGENCY. Of course, the publications have to accept your agency first. They will ask for references from clients for whom you have worked, financial statements, etc., etc. A professional agency does all the following for their 15%:

1. Prepares advertising copy.
2. Lays out copy and art work in final form.
3. Purchases advertising space in volume and passes these savings on to you, along with any other special discounts.
4. Targets proper advertising media for each ad.

5.  Schedules ads and continually places them according to the schedule.

An agency I can heartily recommend is:

Mega Media Associates, Stuart Cogen,
    President
9800 Mariposa Ave.
Fountain Valley, CA 92708

They also handle the *hottest* OPPORTUNITY SEEKER mailing lists.

This agency has an ongoing arrangement with a Los Angeles newspaper to purchase a full page ad for only $2,177. The regular rate is $12,678. You would have to place $58,000 of your own ads for your 15% savings to equal the savings on just this one ad. Couple this with their invaluable advice, and it becomes easy to justify using a professional advertising agency.

In Chapter 3, Lesson 4 states that once you can afford to do so, you should delegate 90% of the day-to-day tasks of running your business. Delegate tasks to the appropriate top professionals in each category. Once you are receiving three or four hundred orders a day, it certainly does not make sense for you to spend all day typing orders and shipping books. If you have a knack for writing ad copy, do that instead. Spend time brainstorming as well. Come up with new products, new business acquisitions, and even entirely new concepts.

## Placing an Ad; Camera-Ready Copy

Most publications require final artwork for display ads. Camera-ready copy means that it is ready to be made into the films that printers use for reproduction. The type has to be typeset, the art must be clear, and the layout must have these elements pasted down.

Even if you get as far as producing a rough layout

by yourself, it won't cost too much to convert it to final artwork. But, if you are doing the whole thing, you must be sure you have all the elements.

To have copy typeset, you go to a typesetting shop and give them typewritten copy for every character you want to show up in your ad. You can discuss the sizes and styles of type with them then.

Final artwork should not be a photocopy of a drawing. It should, rather, be the original drawing or a photostat. A photostat can be made from the original drawing if it needs to be reduced or enlarged to fit the exact size of the layout.

If you are using a photograph, it should be a professional quality print. Any areas that need to be cropped should be indicated with a red grease pencil that will not harm the surface of the photograph. Do not cut the photograph yourself.

If you are using color photography, you may need to have color separations made before you submit the ad. This is a process whereby the color in the photograph is separated into its four elements: red, yellow, blue, and black. The advertising coordinator will be able to tell you what you need, and a local printer can help you with the separations.

If you have no experience in pasting up layouts, you will need to get a professional. Why make a mistake so late in the game? Although it is a simple process of gluing the type and illustrations down with rubber cement, you need the correct tools to be sure that everything is exactly straight.

For those who would like to place their own ad, the following advice should be of help:

1. Place a full page ad for best results.
2. Fill the page with hardhitting advertising copy. Words sell; white space doesn't. Use a

three column format.

3. Ask for placement on the right hand page, far forward (in the first thirty pages).

4. Always key each ad in each publication. Your key can be a department number or letter in your address. For the January issue of *Mother Earth News,* you could use Dept. MEN 1, as in the following example:
TPM Publishing
Dept. MEN 1
1266 North Ave.
Burlington, VT 05401

## Record Keeping

How will you know whether your ads are yielding the response you want? When you place different ads in different publications, you need to have a method of determining which ads are drawing the best results. To do this, you must keep accurate records. You have an address key for each ad you place. Use a separate record sheet for each key. At the top of the sheet, put the pertinent information, such as the name and issue of the publication, the date of issue, the cost of the ad, and any other information about the ad itself. The main body of the record sheet may be divided into two categories: inquiries and orders. These, in turn, are separated into date received, number received, and running totals.

The reason why keeping records is important is two-fold. First, you must respond to any orders you receive without getting them mixed up. Second, you need to determine which publications and which advertisements are bringing in the highest responses. Good records will indicate which headlines pull better, which size has a better draw, and which products out of a catalogue have more appeal.

Testing is the best way to achieve results in advertising. Always test before putting out a major advertising campaign in more than one magazine. If your first test yields total sales of at least two times the cost of the ad, repeat the test. The second test will usually bring in about 25% less. If it also brings in total sales close to two times the cost of the ad, you have a sure winner.

For quick test results, use a newspaper such as *Weekly World News* or the *Los Angeles Herald Examiner*. If your test works in either of these newspapers, it will most likely pull well in other similar media, such as a section of *Family Weekly* or a *Parade* Sunday supplement. Try a "Junior" page ad (7"x10") for your first test. The smaller size will save you money and bring in almost as many orders as a full page (13"x20") newspaper ad.

## Synergism

Synergism is the phenomenon by which separate and distinct processes interact to bring about a result greater than what could be obtained from the sum of the individual processes. It is a wealth-building principle you should know about and use whenever possible. For example, placing twenty space ads simultaneously has a compounding effect on the total response. Were you to place ads successively in twenty different magazines, one a month for twenty months, you would not get the same results as from twenty ads placed simultaneously. Likewise, a direct mail offering coupled with space advertising is usually more effective than the total of both campaigns had they been run at different times. This is a snowballing effect. Constant repetition yields eventual recognition. Recognition prompts curiosity. Readers see an ad repeated everywhere and finally decide to read it through. Repetition builds familiarity and trust. One day, even the most skeptical reader just sits down and orders the product. Magazine space ads complement each other. It doesn't really matter from which magazine a particular order came.

Many advertisers repeat an ad for three consecutive months before "resting" a month. If the response from an ad begins dropping sharply, switch it to another magazine. After a year, change the ad itself.

Magazine ads have an amazingly long life. Orders continue to trickle in months and even *years* after the publication date. Some magazines are rarely thrown out. Have you ever sat in the waiting room of a doctor's office? You might end up reading a 2 year old *Elks Magazine.* An ad catches your eye, and you order the product. Are you going to notice that the magazine is 2 years old and that the advertiser has already retired? No, probably not.

Direct mail solicitation has almost as long a lifespan. We did a mailing of 100,000 on Oct. 11, 1983, and we were still getting an average of 8 orders a day three months later. For a $15 product, that comes to over $100 in sales daily for practically no effort.

Synergism also occurs when you have sold 100,000 books through space advertising, and the *Today Show* asks you for an interview. Shortly after that, one of the largest bookstore chains, Walden Books, asks you to distribute your books through their stores. Continued space advertising, now directing customers to their local Walden Book Store, catapults sales ever upward — to *Best Seller* status. Suddenly, sales are in the stratosphere.

Don't laugh! It happens all the time, especially

with music groups. The recording industry has this process down to a fine art. They are synergistic virtuosos. A band records an album. High pressure promotion results in its being played at 150 radio stations throughout the country. The whole industry charts record sales like fanatics. Public airing of the album increases sales. The band goes on tour. Recognition and sales multiply. The band makes a video. It gets shown on the television show *Solid Gold*. As sales approach the Top Ten, the pace picks up even more. An album selling a million copies has just become reality.

IDEA: Why not create and produce your own cassette tapes with information desired by everyone and promote them using the principle of synergism?

In the next chapter, we will examine this and other new business ideas.

## MAILING LIST COMPANIES

Adco List Management Services     (212) 697-4630
600 Third Ave., New York, NY 10016

Accredited Mailing Lists, Inc.     (212) 889-1180
3 Park Ave., New York, NY 10016

Direct Media, Inc.     (914) 937-5600
90 South Ridge St., Port Chester, NY 10573

Select List Corporation     (516) 676-7831
21 Brewster, St., Glen Cove, NY 11542

Zeller & Letica, Inc.     (800) 221-4112
15 E. 26th St., New York, NY 10010

Business Mailers, Inc.                    (312) 943-6666
640 N. LaSalle St., Chicago, IL 60610


Dependable Lists, Inc.                    (202) 452-1092
1825 K St., N.W., Washington, DC 20006


SRDS Direct Mail List Rates and Data (800) 323-8079
5201 Old Orchard Room, Skokie, IL 60077


Alan Drey Company, Inc.                   (312) 346-7453
333 North Michigan Ave., Chicago IL 60601


BoardRoom Lists                           (212) 239-9000
330 West 42nd St., New York, NY 10036


W.S. Ponton, Inc.                         (412) 782-2360
5149 Butler St., Pittsburgh, PA 15201


PCS Mailing List Company                  (617) 531-1600
125 Main St., Peabody, MA 01960


The Coolidge Company, Inc.                (212) 730-5678
25 West 43rd St. N., New York, NY 10036


Dunhill International List Co., Inc.      (212) 686-3700
381 Park Ave. South, Suite 904, New York, NY 10016


List America, Inc.                        (202) 265-7815
1766 Church St., N.W., Washington, DC 20036

2711 Toledo St., Torrance, CA 90503   (212) 328-9623

## BEST PUBLICATIONS FOR MAIL ORDER ADVERTISING

Write to the appropriate magazine for selling your product and request their advertising media kit. This kit will detail the magazines' circulation figures, cost of a full page ad in black & white, lead time for placing an ad and cost per thousand of circulation.

American Business
1775 Broadway
New York, NY 10019

The Atlantic
Atlantic Monthly Co.
8 Arlington St.
Boston, MA 02116

Income Opportunities
380 Lexington Ave.
New York, NY 10017

Ebony Johnson Publishing
Co., Inc.
820 S. Michigan Ave.,
Chicago, IL 60611

Success
Success Unlimited Inc.
401 N. Wabash
Chicago, IL 60611

Salesman's Opportunity
6 N. Michigan Ave.
Suite 1405, Chicago, IL 60602

Changing Times
Kiplinger Wash. Editors, Inc.
1729 H Street, N.W.
Washington, D.C. 20006

The STAR
News Group Publications, Inc.
730 Third Ave.
New York, NY 10017

Good Housekeeping
959 8th Ave.
New York, NY 10019

Better Homes & Gardens
Locust at 17th
Des Moines, IA 50336

Mother Earth News
105 Stoney Mountain Rd.
Hendersonville, NC 28791

Parade
750 Third Ave.
New York, NY 10017

Money
Time & Life Bldg.
Rockefeller Ctr.
New York, NY 10020

Official Detective Group
235 Park Ave.
New York, NY 10003

Road & Track
1499 Monrovia Ave.
Newport Beach, CA 92663

Wall Street Journal
22 Cortlandt St.
New York, NY 10007

Saturday Evening Post
1100 Waterway Blvd.
Indianapolis, IN 46202

National Enquirer
600 South East Coast Ave.,
Lantana, FL 33464

Money Making Opportunities
Success Publishing
International
11071 Ventura Blvd.
Studio City, CA 91604

Field & Stream
1515 Broadway
New York, NY 10036

Family Weekly
641 Lexington Ave.
New York, NY 10020

Time
1271 Avenue of the Americas
New York, NY 10022

New York Times Magazine
229 W. 57th St.
New York, NY 10036

OMNI
909 Third Ave.
New York, NY 10022

Mechanix Illustrated
1515 Broadway
New York, NY 10022

Penthouse
909 Third Ave.
New York, NY 10022

Popular Science
380 Madison Ave.
New York, NY 10017

INC.
38 Commercial Warf
Boston, MA 02110

Cosmopolitan
224 West 57th St.
New York, NY 10019

Spare Time
5810 W. Oklahoma Ave.,
Milwaukee, WI 53219

Specialty Salesman
6285 Barfield Rd.
Atlanta, GA 30328

Financial Opportunities
4035 W. Dempster St.
Skokie, IL 60076

Venture, The Magazine for
Entrepreneurs
Venture Magazine, Inc.
35 W. 45th St.
New York, NY 10036
(212) 840-5580

Entrepreneur
2311 Pontius Ave.
Los Angeles, CA 90064

MONEYSWORTH
251 W. 57th St.
New York, NY 10019

Psychology Today
One Park Ave.
New York, NY 10016

Globe
1440 St. Catherine W. #625
Montreal, QU Canada H3G1S2

# CHAPTER 8
# Six New Million Dollar Business Plans

Before we start, let me point out that "nothing is new under the sun". We can use new technology or juggle techniques for buying and selling, but it all boils down to buying and selling a product or service.

If you imagined a mysterious stone that turns water into oil by merely dropping it into the water, now is the time to stop deluding yourself. The closest thing to a money-making miracle of which I am aware is a new invention by a backyard "original thinker". The device consists of electromagnets that rotate when a small current is applied. It is reported to produce *ten times* the power it consumes. The patent office will not patent it, despite testimony from reliable scientists that it actually works. Does it work? I don't know. If it does, you need look no further for your miracle money-maker. Simply invest all you have with the person who owns the patent and puts it into production!

But enough of pipe dreams and miracles. We will now examine six businesses anyone can start for little or next to nothing and earn a hefty income.

**MILLION DOLLAR PLAN #1** Sell a Fairytale

There are 20 million children under the age of six in the United States. Without exception, every one of them loves a lullaby or a fairy tale. Here is just the magical ingredient that will make bedtime a pleasure for both child and parent. How? Provide cassette tapes, each containing 30 four minute lullabies and/or bedtime stories. Use a two hour tape, one hour to a side. Sell one new tape each month to your clients. At $10 per tape, some would purchase just one tape. Others would go ahead and order the complete set of 12 tapes at the *special price* of just $59.95.

The beauty of this business is its simplicity. Tapes can be purchased wholesale in large quantities for 50¢ or less each. There are hundreds of fairy tales and lullabies in existence, most of which are in the public domain. This means that no permission is required to use them. If you are creative, you can even write short bedtime stories yourself. You could also team up with an established childrens' writer or hire a talented, but unknown, writer.

If you have a pleasant speaking voice, you can narrate your own tapes. The latest tape recorders will copy your original tape, producing a slow, but steady, supply of product to sell. If your home recording equipment cannot cope with the number of cassettes needed, there are recording studios that will run off 10,000 tapes at a time.

Sell new tapes every month. You can select winter stories for the winter months, or pick appropriate topics for each month, such as Christmas stories for December, etc. Other stories of continuing interest are those of children facing and overcoming hardships. You can also tell inspirational stories, sad stories, or stories of love and friendship. You must have gotten the idea by now. If I go on much farther, I might as well write the stories for you!

## Selling the Tapes

Use classified ads, space ads, or direct mail solicitation. Target publications likely to be read by parents. Sell to parents, day care centers, churches, or babysitters. This is a vast market. If you come up with a quality product, i.e., great uplifting stories that will fascinate a child and please any parent, there is no way you can go wrong.

## Videotapes

Kodak has shaken up the video camera world by coming out with a five pound, hand-held video camera that uses 8 mm videotape on cassettes. You can record a scene, and, with the proper accessories, get instant playback on your television set. Kodak expects to sell 100,000 of these video cameras this year. VCR's (the devices that play video cassettes and video discs) are already selling in the millions. Here is a tremendous untapped market that will grow at astounding rates during the next five years.

**MILLION DOLLAR PLAN #2** Produce and Sell
Video Cassettes

Market low cost video cassettes depicting courses in karate, aerobics, home carpentry, painting, cooking, dancing, child rearing, or virtually any topic that has mass appeal and would especially benefit from a visual display.

Beginner's courses in karate, for instance, are an ideal use for video players. Students attend class and are taught patterns (choreographed punches, blocks, and kicks). Patterns are complicated and difficult to remember. The student does well in class by observing the instructor. Once home, however, practice can be difficult.

Karate studios would purchase tapes covering all nine patterns that are required to advance to Black Belt. Students could check out the appropriate tapes for guidance when practicing at home.

## Best Selling Topics

Physical fitness is in vogue today. Produce and market a videotape of an aerobics workout. Use the soundtrack from best-selling dance albums, with permission from the record companies, of course. Sell several tapes, including beginner, intermediate, and advanced workouts. Produce a videotaped course in yoga. Produce a videotape of a home woodworking project, or perhaps one showing the preparation of unusual foods. While we're dealing with the domestic arts, why not produce cassettes giving instruction in knitting, crocheting, embroidery, leathercraft, candlemaking, pottery, etc.? You can do literally anything along these lines. One person I know sells a videotaped course on *Diamond Appraising*. It sells for $145 each.

Paul Thomas, author of *Psycho-Feedback,* offers a three week, six hour course on videotape. He leases the course materials (including videotapes) to selected instructors throughout the country. He charges (when last I heard) $1,500 to each instructor for the use of his course for one year. Each instructor charges $300 per student taking the course. Five new students are signed up each week, on the average. Classes of approximately fifteen students are held weekly at the instructor's home or school. This gives each instructor gross earnings of $1,500 a week. He is glad to pay the annual leasing cost of $1,500, which enables him to earn up to $78,000 a year, less expenses.

This is peanuts compared to Mr. Thomas' projected income. Were he to present his Psycho-Feedback course offer to 100,000 potential instructors (using direct mail), and if just 1% took him up on his offer to lease his videotaped course for $1,500 annually, his gross income would come to 1½ *million* dollars a year. That's not a bad income for recording a single saleable course on videotape!

*You can do the same!* As an example, consider the karate course mentioned above. It is not necessary for you to develop your own course, as Mr. Thomas did. You are probably not a Black Belt anyway. There is no need. Simply locate a top ranking Black Belt level karate instructor. Pay him a nominal amount (or nothing at all) for the privilege of videotaping the nine patterns plus step by step demonstrations of all the various stances, punches, blocks, and kicks used in a beginner or intermediate course. In return, offer the karate school the following:

1. A complete set of video tapes for their own use.
2. The right to lease or sell tapes to their own students. You sell additional tapes to the school at wholesale.
3. Promise him that his school and the Black Belt instructor himself will receive free advertising on all tapes you produce and sell.

The free advertising could expand his business dramatically. The teacher knows that at the intermediate and advanced levels, there is *no* substitute for one-to-one instruction and practice. Videotapes can never replace him. They can only promote his school and assist his students.

You can either buy the necessary equipment and

"shoot" the course yourself, or hire an agency to make the tapes. The agency will probably produce a more professional product. The money you didn't have to spend on your equipment helps offset the cost of a professional videotaping crew. Once your course has been edited, titled, and completed to your satisfaction, the time has come to market it.

Sell your course to karate schools using space advertising in karate and self defense magazines and by direct mail solicitation. Price the course materials high enough to allow you at least ten to fifteen times as much as their cost of production. You can duplicate your own tapes at home, using your own equipment. Your only expense is the tape itself. This is the ideal way to proceed when you are testing your promotion. If a test ad results in fifteen orders, you simply run off fifteen tapes and ship them.

If your marketing is successful, figure that you will sell 2,500 courses at $250 per course. As an added bonus, you can arrange to give each school that purchases a course a 40% commission on each course they sell. They sell your course to a student for $250 retail and pocket $100 for themselves. You sell them to the schools for $150 wholesale. Think of how many courses you might sell if you had 2,500 studios of self defense acting as your sales agents! If 2,500 studios average only 2 courses sold per month, you are selling 5,000 courses per month at the wholesale price of $150. That comes to total sales of $750,000 per month! Even if just 15% of the projected sales actually materialized, you would be a millionaire before the end of the year.

## Specific Steps to Follow This Plan to a Million Dollars

1.   Purchase karate magazines and visit karate

schools. Check your competition and the need for the product.
2. Contact a karate instructor, and arrange to videotape his course.
3. Contract with a videotaping crew to professionally tape the course. You might get this work done for little or nothing by contacting local colleges and universities. A class might take it on as a learning project.
4. Prepare space advertising and a direct mail package to sell the course.
5. Rent a mailing list of karate schools nationwide.
6. Test your mailing package by mailing to a random selection of the karate schools.
7. Test your space advertising by running an ad in a popular self defense magazine.

## Computers for Fun and Profit

By 1994, computers will take over the majority of teaching functions in our schools. As prices plummet and "user friendliness" increases, computers will become as ubiquitous as TV sets. Eventually, the whole structure of industry will be altered, as more and more of the work force stays home to operate its personal computers. Home-based personal computers tied in with central, main-frame computers, will enable engineers, for example, to work at home. As a result, traffic congestion will ease, and working people will be able to spend more time with their families. Some people will choose to live a town or two away from their employers, perhaps stopping in at headquarters just once a week. For those willing to anticipate the future and accept the challenge, computers hold the key to a prosperous future.

# The Computer — A Tool for Making Money

Computers can be applied to both old and new businesses to handle difficult or time-consuming, repetitive chores. Prior to the computer, mailing lists were alphabetized and stored by hand. Now, a computer can quickly find a customer's name using the order date, his mailing address, or his order number. Using a computer, a business will have no more lost customers because a filing clerk misfiled a name.

A good way to make money with computers is to develop means (called programs or software) of utilizing a computer's capabilities in original, need-fulfilling ways. The next two Million Dollar Plans are examples of this concept. Try to think of other examples yourself.

**MILLION DOLLAR PLAN #3** Form a National Credit Bureau

Presently, there are numerous local and regional credit information agencies. What is needed is a nationwide agency that is capable of recording and storing names and account numbers of customers who issue bad checks. Mail-order businesses in the United States gross $140 *billion* a year. Bad checks account for 1½ to 2% of that total. Businesses lose about $2.5 billion annually to bad checks.

If there were a central clearing house of bad checking accounts that could be accessed by computer, businesses could type in the name, bank account number, and dollar amount of the check for almost instantaneous approval. Names with a previous history of issuing bad checks would be rejected. Participating businesses would pay an annual access fee, which would give them the right to access the central computer in order to pre-approve checks. They would be required to report each bad check received during the year to the National Credit Bureau. They would also be required to send in a photocopy of each bad check in order to safeguard against abuses. These checks would be stored on microfilm, indexed by account number, and added to the central computer's files of bad checks.

A customer could clear his name by making good on all of his bad checks on file. Failure to honor his checks would cause him to be blacklisted by all participating businesses unless he paid by credit card, money order, cashiers check, or cash. In addition to the fees received from businesses for the right to access its files, the National Credit Bureau would retain 10% (or other acceptable fee) of the funds recovered to clear bad checks. The bad account would also be levied a $5 service charge for each bad check. Banks are commonly charging a $2 to $10 bad check charge to the company or individual *receiving* the bad check. This service charge would help to defray the bank's charge to the business, as well as penalize the check bouncer.

The bureaus would derive income by charging each participating business a fifty dollar annual membership fee, which would provide them with access to the central computer. The bureaus would also accept reimbursement for bad checks on behalf of the victimized firms. It would retain 10% of the money it recovers, and would forward the balance to the firms.

This business can be started in a large metropolitan area and then gradually expanded, city by city, until it becomes nationwide. On the local level, it will gross fifty to one hundred and fifty thousand dollars a year. On the national level, income would be in the millions.

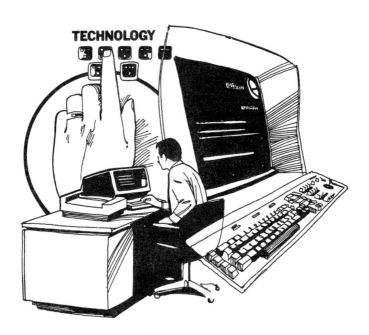

**TECHNOLOGY**

## How to Get Started

Lease or purchase a computer with an initial storage capacity of at least 100,000 names, which can be expanded as the need arises. This should cost about $8,000 if purchased or about $300 a month if leased.

Contact all the banks in your region. Explain that you are forming a central clearing-house of all bad checking accounts, i.e., accounts with a history of worthless checks. Prepare a sales letter and brochure on your business. Offer free membership to each bank in return for its cooperation. Have each bank submit a list of "problem" accounts for inclusion in your master file. Offer the banks something for their trouble — perhaps 1% of the recovered funds from bad checks drawn on their bank.

Send your advertising package to all local businesses, especially those who have received a bad check drawn on a local bank. Remember, the banks have already given you that information. Sign up 4,000 businesses the first year at $50 per membership, which comes to a gross income of $200,000. After deducting the costs of buying or leasing your computer, hiring computer programmers, advertising costs, and other necessary expenses, you are still left with a sizeable profit. Preliminary checking with local businesses showed widespread enthusiasm for this concept. All agreed, including the banks, that a solution to the chronic bad check problem is sorely needed.

## Expand Rapidly Through Multilevel

A way to expand membership rapidly is to employ multi-level promotion. If each new member firm were given the opportunity of making money by recruiting new memberships as well as the benefit of safeguarding its own income, expansion would be multiplied enormously. Every mail-order firm in the United States has a compelling need for this service. Many firms already sell their products to other firms. They can include multilevel membership applications to *The National Credit Bureau* in every mailing they send out. The fifty dollar membership fee could be divided as follows for a five level structure:

| | Commission % by Level | | | | |
|---|---|---|---|---|---|
| **Level** | 1 | 2 | 3 | 4 | 5 |
| **%** | 10.6 | 7.6 | 5.6 | 3.6 | 2.6 |
| **Cash Amount per membership sold** | $5.30 | $3.80 | $2.80 | $1.60 | $1.30 |

Total commissions paid out on any membership sale are 30%, or $15, for each $50 membership.

A firm that sold ten memberships would earn $53

up front, which is enough to cover its own membership fee. But that's not all! If each of those ten new members signed up ten more members, the *second level* earnings would be 10 new members x 10 sales each x $3.80 per sale = $380. At the *third level*, each of these 100 members signs up 10 new members. Income from these sales would be 100 members x 10 sales each x $2.80 per sale = $2,800. At the *fourth level*, each member signs up 10 new members. The *fourth level* earnings are 1,000 members x 10 sales each x $1.80 per sale = $18,000. By the time you reach the *fifth level*, you have 10,000 members, each of whom signs up 10 new members. *Fifth level* earnings would be 10,000 members x 10 sales each x $1.30 per sale = $130,000! Our original sponsoring firm has just made a theoretical $151,233 after selling just ten memberships!

As the creator of the plan, you have the *most* to gain. The combined multilevel sales from just one firm selling the membership to ten others and so on for five levels results in your National Credit Bureau signing up 111,110 new members at $50 each. After paying out 5 levels of commissions, your gross income would be a hypothetical $3,888,885, since you keep $35 for each membership sold.

We say hypothetical because multilevel *never* has a 100% participation rate. Some firms will purchase the $50 membership, but elect not to attempt to sell memberships to others. The main point is that this is the *fastest* way to sign up the most businesses. The more businesses participate, the more effective the National Credit Bureau concept becomes. Your computer will be an absolute necessity in this business. Not only does it keep records of all memberships and all bad checking accounts, but it also handles the entire multilevel program, using one of the new computer programs specifically designed for that purpose.

**MILLION DOLLAR PLAN #4** Develop and Sell Software

Software refers to the prepackaged instructions that program a computer to carry out a particular task. Your Atari cartridge is a piece of software. It instructs your computer to play PAC-MAN with you. Other software directs a computer to store and retrieve mailing lists, do financial projections, edit letters and books, maintain inventory and pricing records, etc., ad infinitum. Almost anything that a person's mind can do can be done by a properly programmed computer. Computers can do tasks that the human mind could neither cope with nor dare attempt. For example, a computer can instantaneously plot the trajectory of a missile in flight and predict its exact landing spot to within a few feet.

The market for software is exploding. People think of many new uses for computers every day. Each new application has to be developed into a computer system, or flowchart, which is then translated to one of the many computer languages by a computer programmer, and stored on a disc or cassette. Copies of this disc or cassette are the new software, which is then marketed.

I am not recommending that you quit what you are doing and train to become a computer programmer. I *do*, however, recommend that you familiarize yourself with computers and use creative imaging techniques to think of new uses for the computer. When you think of a new program idea, check it out. Find out if there is anything similar on the market. If there isn't any program similar to yours, check the marketability of your idea. Will you be able to sell enough programs to justify the expenses of development? Is your idea really needed, or is it just a novelty?

Assuming that it checks out favorably, your next step is to hire a programmer to develop your idea into an actual program, or software. Depending on the genius of your programmer and the complexity of your idea, developing the program could take anywhere from 2 weeks to 6 months of the programmer's time to complete. These people do not work cheaply, so present your idea to him as clearly as possible, and have him give you an estimate of the approximate time and expense needed to complete it.

He will also be the source of input on the merits of your idea. Most knowledgeable programmers can tell you whether your idea has value and, possibly, give you some tips to improve it. Be sure to hire a programmer with integrity. If you have an absolutely brilliant, million dollar idea, you do not want to end up holding smoke while your programmer peddles his program to a multinational for big bucks. It might be wise to have an attorney draw up a performance contract, making all the programmer's work proprietary information. Proprietary information is simply confidential information solely for the use and benefit of the employer, namely you. Once you have a tested, workable program, you must copyright it. Do not skip this step! It is your protection in the event that somebody likes your program and decides to market it for himself. With your program safely copyrighted, it is time to sell it. I recommend offering it to an already established firm with excellent sales outlets for software. If they don't have a program even close to yours in scope or nature, so much the better. This is where your idea turns into money.

You should ask for several times the development costs of the program up front. You should also get a royalty or percentage of all sales. As an example, a word processing program might retail for $250. The manufacturer sells it wholesale for $150. You have negotiated a royalty agreement for 5% of all sales, so your share amounts to $7.50 per unit sold. The first year, they sell 5,000 programs, and you pocket $37,500. The second year, sales jump to 22,000 units. You earn $165,000! By the fourth year, sales have started to trickle off as new, more advanced programs come into being. But, by that time, you have earned over a quarter of a million dollars from one idea alone. In addition, if you are on the ball, you will have developed one or two NEW programs each year.

Impossible? Not at all. A former service station owner started playing with computers a few years ago. Recently, he perfected a couple of outstanding list management programs, which he sells through mail-order for $900. His name is Fred Morrow, and he can be contacted at:

> Green Mountain Computer Services
> Prindle Corners
> Charlotte, VT 05445.

There are always experts who can take your ideas from thought to finished product. Most are only too happy to take their $15 an hour and leave the glory to you. Note that it would take them almost six years of constant labor to earn what you can carn from one idea.

*Bonus Million Dollar Idea.* This idea is a "freebie", and it will work only once — so, first come, first served! Contact the makers of the game Trivial Pursuit. This game outsells Monopoly! It has made millionaires of its inventors, three men from Canada: Scott Abbott, Chris Haney, and John Haney. Parker

Brothers expects to sell 10 to 20 million copies at $30 each next year. Computerize the game Trivial Pursuit, so that it will play on any Atari or other home computer or game system. Since the game is already copyrighted, you will have to negotiate carefully with Parker Brothers in order to be able to convert it to software. With any luck, you should be able to earn 5% of Trivial Pursuit cartridge sales! Remember, you heard it here first.

**MILLION DOLLAR PLAN #5** Shoppers' Monthly

A variation on the information products concept is to publish a resource booklet detailing the best and least expensive sources for all kinds of goods and services a person in your community would want. For instance, I drive a car with a diesel engine, and I have often wondered which stations carry diesel fuel at the lowest price. Haven't you ever had a TV break down and had no idea which service agent provides the most honest and reliable repair service at the least expense? Your booklet will provide the public with answers to questions like these!

The information and format are easily obtained. Simply consult the yellow pages of your telephone directory and begin calling or visiting listings of basic goods and services which are of interest to the public. Ask identical questions at each type of store. For grocery stores, you might compile a list of 20 common foods, such as 1 gallon of milk, 16 oz. orange juice, 1 dozen grade A large eggs, 8 oz. Maxwell House instant coffee, etc. Compare the total prices charged at each grocery store. Then list the top five (by region, if your city is large) in order of prices, with the least expensive store being number 1. Show the comparative prices, and describe the exact product or service as well.

Organize the data you collect into categories, and never compare apples with oranges. In other words, you do not compare the price of a tuneup on a VW at one shop with that on a Cadillac at another. If the second shop does not do work on VW's, perhaps you should have a separate category for American-made cars. You will want to include an index with related categories next to each other. For example, under HOME OWNER SERVICES AND SUPPLIES, you might list the cheapest fuel oil dealers, then the cheapest coal dealers, then the cheapest wood dealers — you get the picture. You will want to spice up the bare facts with anecdotes and special recommendations. For instance, a review of a fine meal at a particularly good restaurant can make an exciting feature article. Besides, you and your family can have a lot of tax-deductible fun reviewing assorted restaurants and movies.

Another invaluable service you can perform is being a consumer watchdog for shoddy or fraudulent business practices. We know of an exposé on a TV repair service which had been systematically and deliberately bilking the public for years. Service employees had been instructed never to leave any service call without coming up with at least $65 in repairs, regardless of the severity of the problem — EVEN FOR AN UNPLUGGED TV SET! They were finally exposed by a newspaper article.

Many automobile repair stations have an underground word of mouth infamy. A few people "in the know" are aware that they are "rip offs". By spreading the word (only after careful and thorough investigation), your publication could save consumers thousands of dollars and much grief. In the process, your booklet will become indispensible to the shoppers in your area. A few such reviews and exposes can result in all the promotion you need to sell thousands of copies.

Once you have typed all your raw information into an interesting format, you must design a simple cover and come up with a title. It is best to use 5½" x 8½" booklet size with a saddle stitched (stapled) cover of slightly heavier stock. A two color, or even a one color, cover is adequate. Keep it simple and inexpensive. The overall length will be determined by the volume of information you have compiled. At any rate, you know where to get it printed for the lowest cost. You have comparison shopped for printers — right? A booklet of less than 50 pages should cost less than 50¢ per copy. In volume of 20,000 or more, that cost can drop to 25¢ or even less. It should be easy to convince your printer to print your first run on 100% credit. Just explain that you will be printing large volumes of booklets each month, and he will want to jump on the bandwagon. Additionally, you can offer him free advertising until circulation hits 20,000 or so. This is too good a deal for him to pass up.

What do you use for a title page? See how you like the example on the next page.   You can charge anywhere from $1.50 to $3.00 for your booklet, depending on its scope.

One money-making avenue that will help increase circulation dramatically is to offer FREE private classified advertising. After all, people interested in bargains will eagerly seek a publication with best buys in commercial products and services as well as private merchandise sales.

Free shopping guides are becoming increasingly popular all over the country. They derive all their profits from commercial advertising. Rates for commercial advertising depend mainly on circulation —

# The *Absolute*

# BEST BUYS

## in ALL of

### ————.
(your city)

*SAVE MONEY

*SAVE TIME AND FUEL SHOPPING AROUND

*AVOID AGGRAVATION — KNOW AT ONCE
WHERE TO GO FOR THE BEST SERVICE
AND THE BEST PRICES!!!

All the BEST SOURCES for absolutely
**EVERYTHING,** updated monthly.

137

the larger the circulation, the higher the advertising rates and revenue. If your community does not yet have a free classified weekly, you might consider incorporating one into your publication.

The least expensive way to distribute your booklets at first is to contact a civic or fraternal organization, such as the Boy Scouts or the Kiwanis. Arrange for them to sell your booklets on a commission basis of 25¢ per copy. Have them pick the copies up directly from the printer and store them until all are sold. At the same time, you should contact your local television and radio stations, extolling the virtues of your fabulous new booklet. Your local Chamber of Commerce may be willing to endorse your booklet as a valuable community resource. Even the local newspaper might be willing to do an article or review of your booklet. Once free promotion is in gear, you might consider employing the space advertising techniques learned in Chapter 6 to sell copies directly to your customers through the mails.

Is it worth the time and effort? How long and how hard would you be willing to work to make $50,000? How about $50,000 a month? The picture of your expenses and sales could well be as follows:

*Sales*
|  |  |  |
|---|---|---|
| 25,000 @ $3 | = | $75,000 |

Expenses
| Cost of printing |  |  |
|---|---|---|
| (25,000 @ $.50) | = | $12,500 |
| Cost of selling |  |  |
| (25,000 @ $.25) | = | $ 6,250 |
| Total expenses | = | $18,750 |

*Profit*

| Sales | | = | $75,000 |
|---|---|---|---|
| Total expenses | | = | $18,750 |
| Profit | | = | $56,250 |

Allow yourself 30 days to gather and compile the information, 21 days for the printer to print the booklets, and 45 days to sell them. In about 3 months, you could be about $56,250 richer with little or no up front cash investment. Depending on the size of your city, you may sell more or less than 25,000 copies your first time out. A large metropolitan area may call for several editions and may sell 50,000 copies of each edition! Burlington, Vermont, is a city of 50,000, with another 50,000 in the surrounding towns in the county. A local shopping guide, here, has a circulation of over 50,000. How many can you sell in your community?

Incidentally, my printer, The Offset House, 1205 Airport Parkway, South Burlington, Vermont 05401, (802) 863-6853, does all my printing on credit. I pay them two weeks to a month AFTER receiving my materials. Other printers are eager for your business and will give you the same terms.

Naturally, you don't want to stop with just one issue. Prices change constantly, new competition moves in, and the public clamors for NEW, UPDATED information. Publish an updated version monthly, with new reviews, new prices and low cost winners, and new exposes of businesses to avoid. To make the gathering of this information easier on yourself, I recommend a tear-out card at the end of each booklet, such as the following:

## LET US KNOW YOUR BEST BUY!

We are constantly searching for the best, least expensive sources of virtually everything. Let us know your best buy of the month, and if we use it, your next copy of Absolute Best Buys of _____ will be sent to you FREE!

### MY BEST BUY THIS MONTH WAS:

Category: _____

Item: _____

Price:_____

Where purchased: _____

Any additional comments, such as bargain days, matinee specials, best person to deal with, etc., are greatly appreciated!

_____

_____

_____

On the other side of this form, include an order form so that customers can order their next copy directly from you. You should also offer an annual subscription for, say, half the newstand price. People looking for bargains will snap up this offer and guarantee you a large, steady income. If just 10,000 people purchase an annual subscription at $18 per subscription, you have generated $180,000 up front. If you sell just 10,000 more copies each month on the newstand or through direct mail, that comes to $30,000 in additional sales each month, for total sales of $540,000 a year.

BUT WAIT! If you are selling upwards of 20,000 copies each month, those very same businesses that are listed in your booklet are going to be enthusiastically placing ads in it. Each page of advertising is worth $250 to $1,000 to you! It costs you but pennies a page to have extras printed. Each page of advertising sold yields tremendous profits.

Realistically, once you have this endeavor off the ground, you can afford to hire experts to do all the advertising layout, information gathering, and type-setting. You can leave the restaurant and movie reviews for yourself — if you still insist on working. START NOW!

**MILLION DOLLAR PLAN #6** Be a Garment Designer-Producer

You may be one of the many people out there who find it necessary to raise a family singlehandedly. Or, perhaps, you are past retirement age and would like to make extra income at home. If you can knit, crochet, embroider, and/or design apparel and other items, such as ski hats, sweaters, mittens, stocking masks (ski masks), socks, etc., you could join the thousands of people doing crafts at home for profit. Most people in this growing field sew for specialty boutiques. Presently, there is a federal law that bans commercial home knitting. Recently, Secretary of Labor, Raymond Donovan, pledged to go to the Supreme Court to reverse this regulation, which dates back to 1942. I expect that by the time you read this book, this archaic law will have been struck down. Please check before you begin in earnest, for your own peace of mind.

Admittedly, for most, this business will never make you a millionaire. However, for those who use the wealth-building techniques in this book, the potential is there. One such person designed unique, luxurious ski caps and distributed them through local department stores. She took pains to give her hats a unique style and expensive feel. All of her products carried her distinctive logo. Pretty soon, her hats "caught on" with the public, and what had been a small cottage business that provided and sold ten hats a day, blossomed into a multimillion dollar apparel designer firm.

## How to Proceed

If you lack knitting or other handicrafting skills, the place to start is in the classroom. People who enjoy working with their hands will pick these skills up quickly. Once you have mastered the basics, it is time to use *creative imaging* techniques to design attractive apparel.

Strive for original designs — offbeat, but attractive. For example, design six different ski bonnets. Also, design a distinctive logo that can be knitted into each garment. Choose a classy, short name. Examples are: Raindeer, Hamil, Provo, Lamplighter, Aspen, and Sterling. If you want to use one of these names, or any other that you may select, you should first check with the United States Bureau of Trademarks and Patents to be sure that the name is not already taken.

Your goal is to design a line of distinctive fashions that are marketable. Use only highest quality materials, and aim at the upper income consumer. You cannot compete with giant manufacturers producing 1,000 caps an hour, each selling for only $3, so aim high. You *can,* however, produce 20 twenty-five dollar hats a day.

Ten years ago, I decided that custom-embroidered shirts and jeans would be a great product. I was right, although the potential has not yet been tapped. My problem was that I didn't even sew, much less embroider. So, I ran a brief classified ad as follows:

*Help Wanted Section*
Work at home embroidering shirts. High cash

earnings for skilled work. No set hours, no quotas — work by the piece. Call Dave at xxx-xxxx for details.

I was deluged with calls. It was a simple matter to interview the applicants and assign each one a test piece to be embroidered.

Those who did quality work and who were satisfied with the compensation offered were given a contract making them *independent contractors*. That way, I was not liable for withholding tax, social security, workman's compensation, insurance, etc., that I would have had to provide for salaried employees. Don't forget this contract. It will keep you out of a quagmire of Department of Labor regulations.

You can hire as many home workers as you need to produce your garments. Start small, and build up an inventory. If sales multiply, you can always hire more home workers. Give each worker a particular design. If you have six different designs, you would have a minimum of six workers. This specialization helps each to become expert at his assigned design, thereby increasing both his speed and net earnings. I suggest offering a bonus for new, unique designs produced by your workers. Fresh ideas are the lifeblood of any business, so reward your people for their creativity.

If you like the embroidered shirt concept, you can purchase shirts directly from the manufacturers in Hong Kong, Singapore, and Korea. Purchase quality garments for next to nothing, have them custom embroidered, and sell them for $30 to $50 each under your own label! You can obtain this information from foreign trade journals, such as:

Taiwan Products Guidance
5 Chung 12th Road
2-1 Street. Shilin
Taipei, Taiwan ROC

Hong Kong Trade Development Council
Hong Kong Enterprise Journal
New York, NY

## Marketing Your Product

Basically, you have two choices to consider. You can either sell your product wholesale to boutiques and department stores or sell retail directly to the consumer, using catalogues. You can begin by lining up several local boutiques to handle your line. I recommend this approach no matter what you eventually do, since their feedback as to pricing, quality, and style will be *invaluable*. This approach will enable you to get your feet wet without taking a cold dunking if you have misjudged the market. Face to face selling will be required. Make appointments with the buyers at the various stores you have selected. Choose expensive boutiques that carry related apparel.

A 100% or greater markup is routine, so pick a suggested retail price and take half, or even less, as your wholesale price. Offer a 10% discount for quantity orders, 25 or more pieces, for instance. Your wholesale price should be at least twice your cost. Thus, if you pay $5 for a ski bonnet made by a home worker, sell it at a wholesale price of at least $10. The shop sells it retail for $19.95 to $24.95.

Once you have tested the market in this fashion, you can decide whether to sell your product wholesale, retail, or a combination of both. If you sell wholesale, be prepared to be swamped with dozens of orders, each one for dozens of products daily. The benefit of selling wholesale is that once you have placed your line of products in a number of boutiques, you should get a continuous stream of large orders. The disadvantages include the headaches of maintaining high production and accepting a lower profit margin for each unit sold.

At any rate, either approach will require that you prepare a catalogue or sales brochure, especially if you intend to use direct mail selling. For wholesale selling, simply prepare a brochure or a 4 to 6 page catalogue with professional drawings of your product(s) accompanied by a typewritten sales letter which includes wholesale and suggested retail price lists. Be sure to plainly show discounts for quantity purchases, shipping costs, and any other factors that would affect the price. Include a BRE and a *free sample* order coupon. The purchasing agent is given the opportunity to examine a sample of the merchandise prior to placing an order. Only those who respond to your offer get the free sample(s). Send another brochure and order form along with the requested sample. If you do a large mailing, you may get a large response, which will cost you numerous sample products. Nevertheless, you have to give a little to get a lot. The orders you derive from this promotional giveaway will repay you many times over.

## Direct Retail Selling

The primary difference here is that you will rent mailing lists, not of boutique owners, but of individuals who have purchased ski wear or fashion apparel. A good list broker can direct you to the appropriate lists. Selling clothing directly to your customers might be more difficult than selling to boutiques and department stores. People like to see, touch, and try on clothing before purchasing. But never doubt that it can be done. L.L. Bean does a booming business. Sears sold clothing through its catalogues longer than any other retailer, and look where they are today!

To be successful, you must build a quality public image, broad recognition, and a reputation for reliable service. Fill orders promptly, and offer a *Solid Money-Back Guarantee.* Gradually expand your line to fill up a small catalogue. If you make and sell "tewks" (knitted ski hats), you might seek the endorsement of a recognized ski racer. A proper endorsement may cost $50,000 to $300,000. Instead, just mail out free samples plus a friendly personal letter to each racer hoping that they will enjoy their new hats. It could get you a free endorsement and great publicity.

## Profit Picture

This is a business that anybody can operate right from his own home, (you don't even have to knit). Profits can range from a couple of hundred dollars a week to unlimited amounts, depending on whether you sell to just a few boutiques or to many large department stores. Using the techniques for promoting your product given in Chapter 7, you could easily earn a thousand dollars a week in profits. Although knitted and embroidered products have been used as examples, this type of business principle could easily be generalized to virtually *any* craft that can be done at home. Other examples are crochet, macrame, leathercraft, and items made of wood.

# CHAPTER 9
# Managing Your
# New-Found Wealth

Until now, I have assumed that you desired to create a large wealth-building income fairly quickly, enabling you to enjoy the benefits of a lifetime of being wealthy. A person with a spendable income in the hundreds of thousands of dollars can "afford" to become wealthy by investing a portion of his income, rather than spending everything. Working for a large income, even $100,000 a year, does not qualify as "having it made" by my definition. To qualify, you must have assets earning this income for you year in and year out, whether or not you work.

I cannot stress strongly enough that starting and owning the right business(es) is the fastest means to your goal. Nevertheless, even those who refuse to leave the so-called "security" of their salaried jobs can eventually become wealthy. It just takes them two or three times as long.

Both entrepreneur business owners and salaried investors must continually invest a portion of their income. The former may invest all but his family's reasonable living expenses back into his own business for the first two or three years. After that, he may continue to take any excess profits generated by his business in order to expand and diversify. His choice is simple. If he feels that he can earn a greater return on his money by creating his own investment opportunities, then he should invest most of his money in his own ventures. Any remaining funds can be placed in diverse assets to protect against business reversals.

The salaried investor, on the other hand, has only one choice, namely where to invest his money. The amount invested should not be less than 10% of annual income. In the higher tax brackets, 20% is not unreasonable, provided that you are serious about retiring wealthy.

## Investment Characteristics

There are some good reasons to invest, other than long-term appreciation of assets.

1.   Invest in *liquid* assets, so that you can convert them to cash quickly and easily. There will always be "here today, gone tomorrow" opportunities where cash is king. I bought four gold coins the other day for $635 *cash*. The seller had to have *cash* by that evening. He had just turned down an offer of $650 because the prospective buyer could only pay by check. My coins were recently appraised for $1,135.

2.   Invest in *portable* assets as security against the unthinkable. Throughout history, people have been suddenly uprooted by forces of political and religious persecution. Refugees have escaped persecution and war with their lifetime savings in a satchel. Prior to World War II, a few sophisticated Jews converted most of their assets to diamonds. They escaped Nazi Germany with the diamonds secreted on their bodies.

3.   Invest in *income producing* vehicles to get

cash flow. Treasury bills, income property, bonds, money market funds, and stocks earn income in the form of interest, dividends, or rents. Bullion, rare coins, fine art, and diamonds produce no income.

4. Invest in assets that are an *inflation hedge*. Few paper investments, such as stocks, T-bills, bonds, etc., are a hedge against inflation. Bullion, rare coins, fine art, and real estate do well in an inflationary economy.

5. *Active* versus *passive* investments. Some investments require intensive research and ongoing management in order to hold them profitably. Your own business is an *active* investment. Real estate is slightly less so. Most other investments require little or no management, once purchased.

6. *Leverage* is the key to making an investment work harder, thereby paying off at a rate several times that of an unleveraged investment. We are all familiar with the concept of buying real estate for 5 or 10% down. That is an example of leverage. Coins, bullion, stocks, and commodities can also be purchased using leverage. Also, don't forget that using other peoples' money to build your own business is simply another use of leverage.

7. *Stable* versus *volatile* investments. Commodity futures, stocks, bullion, and bonds are all relatively volatile investments. Prices may fluctuate daily. Rare coins, real estate, discounted mortgages, and T-bills are all relatively stable. Broad fluctuations in price are rare.

Of the above investment characteristics, power and stability are the most important. Power comes from the use of leverage, from strong forces of supply and demand, and from economic factors, such as inflation. To achieve wealth goals quickly, we must insist on a 25% compounded annual rate of return, or better. Does this sound high, or even nearly impossible? On the contrary, a 25% return is well within range.

Each business strategy reviewed earlier is capable of generating many times this figure. In my publishing business, I expect to take in double my costs each time I do a mailing or an ad campaign. A commodity futures broker telephoned the other day boasting about his firm's unusual record of 400% gains in a year. I replied that it would be unwise for me to divert working capital to risky commodity speculation, since I can double my working capital every couple of months with relatively little risk. Using the principle of leverage by doing much of our mailing on credit, we actually get a 1600% annual return (not compounded). That, of course, is why I say that your own business, along the lines I have described, is the fastest way to a million dollars. Business is somewhat risky, however, and if you lack the time or stomach for it, I believe that your best investment choice is a balanced portfolio of real estate, rare coins, and discounted mortgages.

## Real Estate

Start your investment plan by owning your own home. Paying rent is an inexcusable long-term waste of money. Mortgage payments usually do not exceed by much what the rental would be for the same property. There are hundreds of books telling you how to buy property with little or no down payment. One I recommend is *Nothing Down* by Robert G. Allen, published by Simon and Schuster.

A look at the assets of average Americans shows that most of their net worth is derived from home ownership. Yet few people acknowledge this fact and go on to expand their real estate holdings. Why is real estate such a powerful investment vehicle? The answer is that real estate combines both the *power* of leverage and the *stability* of consistent long-term upward price movements. It is this use of leverage, coupled with stable, steady appreciation that allows real estate investments to consistently outperform other investment vehicles.

To illustrate, assume that we have purchased a duplex for $50,000 with $10,000 down. Assume also that its value goes up 10% each year and that rents cover the mortgage payments plus expenses. Let us examine the growth of our $10,000 investment over a period of three years.

*Initial purchase*

| | | |
|---|---|---|
| Property value | = | $50,000 |
| Mortgage | = | $40,000 |
| Equity | = | $10,000 (our down payment) |

*Status after 1 year* ($500 has been paid to principal, reducing the mortgage.)

*Property value*

| | | |
|---|---|---|
| Original price | = | $50,000 |
| Appreciation (10%) | | |
| | = | $ 5,000 |
| Total value | = | $55,000 |

*Mortgage*

| | | |
|---|---|---|
| Original mortgage | | |
| | = | $40,000 |
| First year payment to principal | | |
| | = | $   500 |
| Remaining mortgage | | |
| | = | $39,500 |

*Equity*

| | | |
|---|---|---|
| Property value | = | $55,000 |
| Mortgage | = | $39,500 |
| Equity | = | $15,500 |

*Status after 2 years* ($564 has been paid to principal, reducing the mortgage.)

*Property value*

Value after 1 year
= $55,000

Appreciation (10%)
= $ 5,500

Total value     = $60,500

*Mortgage*

Mortgage unpaid after 1 year
= $39,500

Second year payment to principal
= $    564

Remaining mortgage
= $38,936

*Equity*

| | | |
|---|---|---|
| Property value | = | $60,500 |
| Mortgage | = | $38,936 |
| Equity | = | $21,564 |

*Status after 3 years* ($635 has been paid to principal, reducing the mortgage.)

*Property value*

Value after 2 years
= $60,500

Appreciation (10%)
= $ 6,050

Total value     = $66,550

*Mortgage*

    Mortgage unpaid after 2 years
               = $38,936
    Third year payment to principal
               = $   635

    Remaining mortgage
               = $38,301

*Equity*

    Property value  = $66,550
    Mortgage       = $38,301

    Equity          = $28,249

Equity is the difference between property value and mortgage balance. After three years, the duplex is worth $66,550. The mortgage has been reduced to $38,301 by the monthly rent payments. Our equity in the house is $28,249, which means that our original $10,000 investment is now worth $28,249. In other words, $10,000 has made $18,249 for us in just three years, for a total gain of 182%. That averages out to a gain of over 60% per year, compounded annually!

Depreciation, mortgage interest payments, real estate taxes, and all maintenance and repairs are tax deductible. Assuming that our investor is in a 30% tax bracket and that these items add up to $7,500 annually, he will save $2,250 on his income tax each year. With figures like these, it is no surprise that real property is the cornerstone of many estates.

## Investment Strategy

For the entrepreneur-businessperson, I recommend that consideration should be given to other long-range investments such as real estate, rare coins, and discounted mortgages only after a net annual income of $100,000 or more has been attained. With 4½ times the income of the average American family, you can afford to invest a disproportionately greater amount. For instance, the median family income is $22,000 a year. Such a family is doing well if it can invest $2,500 annually. This is because they are caught between a rock and a hard place, namely the rock of inflation and the hard place of high taxes. They are actually held down to a comfortable subsistence level.

The self-employed entrepreneur, on the other hand, saves a small fortune in taxes. If he and his family "sacrifice" by spending no more than the average family on consumables, say $19,500, that leaves him $80,500 before taxes, to invest. If he invests just $25,000 a year in real estate, he could well be a millionaire from real estate alone within 9 years, and who knows how much his business would be worth by then.

## Rare Coins

One drawback of real estate is its lack of liquidity. There are many occasions where cash or a close substitute is KING. There are always unexpected expenses as well as unexpected investment bargains cropping up. You cannot afford to be property rich and cash poor in a crisis. That is why I recommend diverting 70% of savings to on-going real estate purchases. Spend 20% on choice, uncirculated or better rare coins. Keep 10% of your assets in money market funds, T-bills, and cash.

Personally, I choose uncirculated United States gold coins as my rare coin investment. Common date Classic Head $5 gold coins of the years 1834 to 1838 showed a 17,500% overall increase in value from 1955 to 1982. An investor who purchased 100 of these coins for $2,500 in 1955 could have resold them in 1982 for $500,000! These particular coins appreciated faster than almost any other coin during the period.

However, their rate of appreciation might slow down during the next 27 years. For this reason, the investor who seeks the assistance of an expert and reliable rare coin dealer will do better than one who relies solely on past performance. The most important things to remember are: 1. be sure to get what you pay for and 2. pay a realistic price.

If a coin is sold as MS 60 (average, uncirculated in original Mint State condition), it is supposed to be an average uncirculated coin. No trace of wear can be evident. The price differential between an AU (About Uncirculated) coin and the same coin in MS 60 condition is vast. More than one grading error can throw an entire rare coin investment program into jeopardy. For this reason, have all rare coin purchases independently appraised. All reputable dealers sell coins on a 10 day approval basis. If the coin is not genuine or if the grade is not that claimed, you may return it. If a particular dealer sent you overgraded coins more than once, find another dealer. Check every coin you purchase. Take nothing for granted.

Some time ago, I purchased two California gold quarter dollars from a good friend. He assured me that they were fine quality, genuine examples, as he had purchased them years ago from an old, established dealer. Because I still had a measure of doubt, I purchased them with the understanding that if they should prove counterfeit, I would get my money back. To my friend's shock and consternation, both coins turned out to be counterfeit.

If you have a questionable coin, you can send it

to American Numismatic Association Certification Service (ANACS). The address is:

ANACS
818 N. Cascade
Colorado Springs, CO 80903
(303) 473-9142.

Coins up to $500 in value will be authenticated for $15 or less and graded as to condition for $6. Also, an ANACS certified coin is easier to sell.

## Pricing of Rare Coins

Like real estate, rare coin prices are relatively stable. Dealers rely to a large extent on the information contained in the *grey sheet*, officially called the *Coin Dealer Newsletter* (P.O. Box 2308, Hollywood, CA 90028). A subscription costs $60 per year. This newsletter is published weekly and updates all collectible coin prices. These are tabulated from the sales of numerous dealers and auctions nationwide.

Prices for each coin are arranged by grade in Bid and Ask columns. Dealers who need particular coins for their inventory offer Bid or close to Bid prices via Telex offerings to other dealers. Retail sales are made at or close to the listed Ask prices. It can be difficult to sell your coins at full Bid prices. Most dealers simply will not pay Bid prices to a retail customer. They usually pay 10 to 25% less than or *back of bid*. This makes shopping around for the best dealer a wise move.

Read *The Official Investors Guide to Gold Coins* by Marc Hudgeons for an informative look at United States gold coins, their past price history, and future potentials. He also has similar books covering silver dollars and United States silver coins. These books are available at $7.95 each, including shipping, from:

TPM Publishing
P.O. Box 3088
Burlington, VT 05401.

## Discounted Mortgages

While real estate is a great wealth builder, it is often difficult to spend your wealth. Frequently, properties have a negative cash flow. They may cost you a few dollars a month more than they generate in rents. You may arrive at a point where you are worth $1.25 million on paper in equities, yet owe another $3 million in mortgages. You have worked hard, sacrificed, yet you certainly don't feel like or live like a millionaire.

Now is the time to generate a comfortable cash income, reduce management headaches to near zero, and reap the benefits. The solution? Transfer your $1.25 million of property equity into *discounted mortgages*. Sell off your holdings, getting the best deals you can. Use your cash to purchase mortgages on the open market which yield 22 to 26% after discounting.

Several years ago, I needed funds to start my own business. I had previously sold some land in California, taking back a second mortgage in lieu of all cash for my equity. I was receiving $175 a month at 10½%. After three years, I would receive a *balloon payment* for the entire remaining balance, about $18,000. Since I needed cash immediately, I could have sold my mortgage at a discount. I would get less than the $18,000 face value in order to receive an immediate cash settlement. The cash offered turned out to be $13,000. The cash generated by this mortgage was to be 36 months of $175 payments plus a balloon payment of $18,000 at the end of three years, for a total of $24,300 in benefits. I had to make the choice of receiving $24,300 over a three year period or $13,000 cash immediately. The potential investor would reap nearly 29% annual return on his $13,000 investment. Many people would have taken the cash gladly. I elected to pledge the mortgage at full face value as collateral for a personal loan at 13% interest. Nevertheless, discounted mortgages are being sold all the time.

## Benefits of Purchasing Discounted Mortgages

A mortgage purchased at discount to yield 24% annually is a wealth perpetuator. Few investments are more secure, more lucrative, and as trouble-free as discounted mortgages.

When purchased at wholesale with yields of 22% to 26%, they can be resold at retail with a yield of 16% to 18%. Were you to pick up my mortgage example given above for $13,000, you could turn around and resell it for $14,294 to a less savvy investor who would be satisfied with a 17% return. You make an immediate cash profit of $1,294.

If the worst happens, and the mortgage defaults, you gain ownership of the property securing the mortgage. If you have done your homework correctly, the property is worth well over the total of your mortgage and any other primary debt (first mortgage). Either rent the property or sell it at a tidy profit.

In the event the property securing the mortgage is sold before the mortgage is paid off, the note will be paid off at *full face value,* resulting in a windfall profit over and above the discounted yield.

## How to Find Them

Relatively few people are aware that these very

secure and high yield investments are available. During the last several years with high interest rates, tight money, and a sluggish real estate market, many home sellers were forced to take back "paper". In other words, they had to hold a second mortgage on the property that they sold. The days of quick and easy bank financing which pays the seller the entire price in cash are gone. Many of these sellers never wanted monthly payments. They would rather take less cash all at once and be done with it.

## Classified Ads

Place an ad in the Financial column of the classified section of your Sunday newspaper. In the ads, "TD" stands for Trust Deed, a common term for second and third mortgages. Examples of such ads are:

Buying seasoned TD's with good equity. Call xxx-xxxx.

Paying CASH now for your well secured TD. Call private investor now at xxx-xxxx.

You may also see a listing for sellers of TD's. Such ads may well read as follows:

Get 25% yield. Purchase $35,000 TD for $22,000. 13% interest, $275/mo for 48 mo. By owner.

Selling 2nd TD secured by fashionable home in good neighborhood. $15,000 required, yields 22%.

Call the sellers to get the following details you need to know:
1. Face value of TD and interest rate
2. Amount of the discount
3. Discounted purchase price of the TD

4. Market value of property and location
5. The remaining balance on the first mortgage
6. Monthly payment and term
7. Annual yield after the discount

With this information in hand, drive past the property for a first-hand inspection. In the event that the current owner of the house defaults, you will have to foreclose. View the property as you would any prospective purchase, for you might end up owning it. If the property is messy and run down, beware. The buyer may also be careless about making his mortgage payments.

## Financial Analysis

If the property itself seems all right, being kept in good order, and apparently worth as much as the seller claims, then it is time to do a financial analysis of the prospective purchase. The calculation of three simple ratios will clarify this. As an example, assume that a mortgage seller holds a $15,000 second mortgage with monthly payments of $165 and interest of 12% per year for twenty years. He is willing to sell it for $9,000 cash, rather than take the monthly installments for the next twenty years. A $95,000 house secures the mortgage, and there is a first mortgage of $35,000.00

*Ratio #1: Ratio of total loans to property value*
Add the first and second mortgages to obtain total loans.

$$\frac{\text{Loans}}{\text{Value}} = \frac{\$50,000}{\$95,000} = 53\%$$

You are looking for a low percentage, below 75%. The

lower the percentage, the more equity to protect you in case of default.

Ratio #2:   Equity to debt ratio
Subtract the total amount of loans from the value of the house to obtain equity ($95,000 - $50,000 = $45,000). Then divide equity ($45,000) by total debt ($50,000).

$$\frac{\text{Equity}}{\text{Debt}} = \frac{\$45,000}{\$50,000} = 90\%$$

A high figure indicates that you are well secured. Avoid percentages below 30%.

Ratio #3:   Discount to debt ratio
The discount is the difference between the face value of the mortgage and the amount the seller asks for it. In this case, the seller is willing to let a $15,000 mortgage go for $9,000. The discount is then $15,000 - $9,000 = $6,000. Divide the discount by the value of the mortgage preceding the discounted mortgage. In this example, this refers to the first mortgage of $35,000.

$$\frac{\text{Discount}}{\text{Debt}} = \frac{\$\ 6,000}{\$35,000} = 17\%$$

Discount is another word for profit in this transaction. Debt is another word for risk, or exposure. If the profit is too low relative to the risk or exposure, the transaction is not worth the risk. Look for discount/-debt ratios over 15%.

In the above example, if the discount were only $2,000, the ratio would be $\frac{\$\ 2,000}{\$35,000} = 5.7\%$. Handling a default and subsequent foreclosure could easily cost $2,000 in attorneys' fees and lost mortgage payments. This makes a 5.7% ratio too low and, therefore, too risky.

If the ratios check out satisfactorily, check the payment record on the second mortgage. Has the mortgagee skipped any payments? Are his payments on time? If the payment record is poor, you may have trouble in the future and find it necessary to foreclose.

The wealthy investor who puts half a million dollars into discounted mortgages yielding 24% derives $120,000 in annual income, whether or not he works. The small business owner who can place just $75,000 of his money into discounted mortgages earns $18,000 a year, whether business is good or bad. Since this is neither a book on real estate or on rare coins, I recommend that you do research into these areas in depth — when you are ready.

# CHAPTER 10
# Look to Your Future — Now

*"To make a great dream come true, the first requirement is a good capacity to dream; the second is persistence — a faith in the dream"*

Hans Selye, M.D.

In this book, I have tried to show you just how important your "mind set" is to your success. Positive thinking alone will probably not make you rich. You must couple positive **Can Do** attitudes with **Action** and then follow a specific, realistic plan to achieve your goal. You have learned that you must first develop a *Mind for Success* in order to effectively choose your goals and implement them. A person with the mind set of a "loser" repels money and success; and — you guessed it — the person with a *Mind for Success* appears to "luck into" one money-making opportunity after another. Believe me, what appears to be sheer luck is really the use of your Mind for Success, developed with the help of this book and used to make money according to the principles given.

To some, the concept that success can be a WIN-WIN game in which every participant comes out feeling like a winner is unbelievable. Understand that if you operate in any other way, success is a mirage, not worth attaining. The WIN-WIN philosophy is a valid wealth-building principle. You make no sacrifices when you practice it; in fact, it helps you. That is because when you honestly look out for your customers' interests, you generate an expanding universe of goodwill that will multiply your business many times over. And the gratitude and affection of those whom you have helped gives you a peace of mind that cannot be purchased at any price.

Hopefully, you now realize that you, and you alone, are responsible for your success or failure, and that the lack of initial capital is no excuse either for a lack of effort at becoming successful or for failure. It surely takes money to make money. Those miracle money-making plans that promise you pie in the sky with no investment are for dreamers only. But you now know ways to raise cash quickly when you need it. You have also seen how the effective use of credit allows you to charge most of your expenses and earn double your costs within a month. This is the next best thing to a no investment business that is realistically attainable.

I have encouraging news for you! You now have what it takes to become wealthy. You now realize that self-education and action are necessary if your dreams are to be realized, or you would not be reading this book. In fact, those of you with a creative imagination are already potentially rich. This is true because the combination of creative, properly directed imagination with active research is the *most potent resource* available to you. Just ONE IDEA, followed by ACTION can make you a millionaire.

You now know the five wealth-building principles that can take anyone from poverty to riches. They have worked too many times in the past to fail anyone with a true commitment to his goal. If you believe, you will succeed.

"The winners in life think constantly in terms of *I can, I will,* and *I am.* Losers, on the other hand, concentrate their waking thoughts on what they should have or would have done, or what they can't do".

Dr. Dennis Waitley

Dr. Waitley was right. You are what you think. You cleanse your body daily; now cleanse your mind. Brainwash yourself! Scrub out all those self-defeating, negative thoughts. Wash out doubt, insecurity, greed and malice. Mark Twain said:

"Keep away from people who try to belittle your ambition. Small people always do that, but the really great make you feel that you, too, can become great."

Cleanse you mind daily with a bath of inspirational thoughts. Right now, go out and get your personal copy of an inspirational book. Read it through, then jot down those phrases you find most poignant. Repeat them to yourself daily — when you go over your *Goal Contract.* Some books I recommend are: *Think and Grow Rich* by Napoleon Hill, *The Bible, The Power of Positive Thinking* by Norman Vincent Peale, and *Psycho-Feedback* by Paul G. Thomas.

Work on developing your own *Mind for Success.* While you are doing that, choose one of my six business plans and **do it!** Don't wait for an invitation — there is no better time to *act* than the present. If you don't like any of the six plans, you can use what you have learned to come up with something even better! I am eager to hear of your successes. Remember, most of you have qualified for a full year's free consultation privileges. Simply write or call, and I will try to give you the benefit of my experience.

Dave Davies
RFD #3
Box 835
Montpelier, VT 05602
(802) 229—4737

**P.S.** - SUCCESS DYNAMICS, INC. produces a complete line of subliminal motivation cassettes designed to help you in your effort to develop a "MIND FOR SUCCESS". Thousands use our tapes to increase their self confidence, creativity and motivation. We have 45 titles, so if you would like to know more send your name and address for our FREE CATALOG. Include $2 if you would like to experience our SUBLIMINAL TEST TAPE. This tape explains the subliminal motivation process and sends you a powerful subliminal message to try our other tapes.

**WRITE:**
FREE CATALOG
SDI
16 STATE STREET
P.O. BOX 1087
MONTPELIER, VT 05602

# A Personal Message
# from the Author

Recently, I came up with a way to enable you to make substantial profits in your own publishing business immediately. You do not have to write a book or any advertising. You do not have to risk large sums of money. In fact, you can spend as little as $1250 to get started. After that, money continues to roll in, building ever larger profits. How much you earn and how much of your profits you reinvest in your business are entirely up to you.

Too often a great idea like writing and selling your own information package doesn't quite work out for two reasons. First, you may not have the time or money needed immediately to write and have your own book published. Just having your manuscript typeset and prepared "camera ready" for the printer usually costs $10 to $15 per page. A 150 page book would cost you $1,500 to have it typeset, plus the expense of having the books printed. The first 1,500 copies of your book could cost you about $3,000. If you have the $3,000 and the ideas and time to research your book, that's not bad - not when you can sell your books for $15 each.

The second requirement is that you have to come up with some great advertising to sell your new book. One very successful advertising copywriter I know charges a flat $5,000 to prepare a "professional" mailing package. OR, you can write it yourself and test it to find out if your sales message will sell enough of your books to be sucessful. A minimum test is a mailing to 5,000 names, but 10,000 or 15,000 is better because that way you can test 2 or 3 different mailing lists as well as your new brochure. The cost of preparing just 5,000 mailing packages (brochure, return envelope, #10 mailing envelope, order form, and, sometimes, a short sales letter), renting a mailing list of 5,000 names, and mailing your brochures is about $1800 if you write and design the package yourself!

Many people, when confronted with these obstacles would have little chance of success starting their own publishing business from scratch.

Since my company, Success Dynamics, Inc. has been successful since day one I decided most entrepreneurs would have the best odds of success if they could follow precisely in my footsteps by selling a proven product, my book MIND OVER MONEY.

Recently I discovered a completely new approach to advertising that reaches a huge and expanding market, works 24 hours a day every day of the year and costs relatively little to use.

NO ONE ELSE TO MY KNOWLEDGE KNOWS OF MY TECHNIQUE OR IS USING IT AS I WRITE THIS!

The concept and the profitable results of using it are so powerful and so effective that I decided to franchise Success Dynamics Distributorships allowing selected franchisees to profit from my methods.

I will not accept everyone for a Success Dynamics Franchise. Nor will I reveal my secret marketing technique here.

What I've done is prepared a video presentation coupled with the actual Success Dynamics Franchise Instruction Manual. This introductory kit will not only tell you but show you exactly how you can earn a great income as our franchisee. The kit itself is NOT DESIGNED TO MAKE YOU MONEY nor is it or can it be a substitute for the actual Success Dynamics franchise.

What it does do is introduce you to my secret marketing concept by showing you the actual instruction manual and training video used by our franchisees.

HERE ARE SOME GUIDELINES TO FOLLOW WHEN CONSIDERING ORDERING OUR INTRODUCTORY FRANCHISE KIT:

1. Don't send for it if you have no permanent address.
2. Don't send for it if you have been irresponsible with your credit. All our franchisees must be mature, credit-worthy individuals.
3. Don't apply if you couldn't or wouldn't invest at least $1500 in your own business. Frankly, I don't have time for dreamers or those incapable of raising and investing the small capital required to get started.
4. Don't apply if you are lazy, dishonest or unmotivated. This may be the easiest to operate franchise in existence but we won't consider people unwilling or incapable of putting out the extra effort!
5. Do send for the kit if you can afford to devote from one hour to 20 hours per week starting and operating your franchise from your home or office.
6. Do send for the kit if you want to earn extra income ranging from $10,000 to unlimited annual profits.
7. Do send for the kit if you've always wanted to own your own business but don't want to re-invent the wheel or incur a lot of risks and headaches getting started.

It takes a certain type of person to successfully run their own business. Successful applicants must understand the relationship of risk to reward and be willing to bet their time, energy and money on their venture.

They must be capable of paying attention to details and following through with action when required. And above all, they must believe in themselves and their ability to succeed!

If you are one of these people and you are interested in learning about my franchise opportunity send $50. for our Success Dynamics Introductory Franchise Kit. Watch the video, review the franchise plan and the secret marketing technique and then you can decide whether to apply for your franchise or return the kit.

You may review the kit for 30 DAYS RISK FREE. If you are not interested simply return it within the 30 Days for a courteous refund.

IF YOU APPLY FOR AND ARE ACCEPTED AS OUR FRANCHISEE THE COST OF THE KIT WILL BE DEDUCTED FROM THE FRANCHISE FEE.

IF YOU APPLY FOR OUR FRANCHISE AND YOU ARE NOT ACCEPTED, WE WILL NOTIFY YOU SO YOU CAN RETURN THE KIT FOR A REFUND AT THAT TIME.

This franchise offer may be withdrawn at any time and for any reason (ie. upon filling our regional quotas) without prior notice.

TO CHECK ON FRANCHISE LOCATIONS STILL AVAILABLE AND TO ORDER YOUR INTRODUCTORY KIT VIA CREDIT CARD

PHONE TOLL FREE
1-800-223-9026 (orders only)
VT residents call 1-802 229-4737

or send the order form to:
SDI
16 STATE STREET
P.O. BOX 1087
MONTPELIER, VT 05602

Note: Money order, cashiers check, cash or credit card orders processed and shipped within 24 hours. PERSONAL CHECKS DELAY ORDER THREE WEEKS.

## 30 DAY GUARANTEE

Review the SDI FRANCHISE OFFER. If not interested return within 30 days for refund. Full cost of FRANCHISE INTRO PACKAGE IS APPLIED TO FRANCHISE COST WHEN FRANCHISE IS PURCHASED WITHIN 30 DAYS OF RECEIPT OF INTRO PACKAGE. APPLICANTS FAILING TO SECURE A FRANCHISE MAY RECEIVE A FULL REFUND WHEN INTRO PACK IS RETURNED WITHIN 30 DAYS OF NOTIFICATION.

Success Dynamics Inc.
16 State St.
Montpelier, Vermont 05602

-------------------- DETACH HERE --------------------

DETACH ALONG DOTTED LINE

# SUCCESS DYNAMICS, INC.

16 State street
P.O. Box 1087
Montpelier, VT 05602

**YES** I wish to evaluate your SDI franchise opportunity. RUSH your SDI INTRODUCTORY FRANCHISE PACKAGE (including video) to me at once. I'm ordering with the understanding that I have 30 DAYS to review the FRANCHISE OFFER RISK FREE and with no further obligation. If not interested, I may return the FRANCHISE PACKAGE within 30 DAYS for a full refund.
IMPORTANT: SPECIFY  ☐ VHS OR  ☐ BETA (video format)

Enclosed is $50.00 in the form of:
☐ I've included $5 extra (total $55) for RUSH FIRST CLASS SHIPPING & HANDLING.
☐ Money Order  ☐ Check  ☐ VISA  ☐ MasterCard  ☐ AMEX  ☐ Cash

My credit card # _____

Expiration Date: _____ Signature _____

Ship to _____

Success Dynamics pays postage & handling. Personal checks delay order 3 weeks.
OFFER VALID ONLY IN THE U.S.
CREDIT CARDS ORDER TOLL FREE: 1-800-223-9026

DETACH ALONG DOTTED LINE

## SUCCESS DYNAMICS, INC.

16 State street
P.O. Box 1087
Montpelier, VT 05602

**YES** I wish to evaluate your SDI franchise opportunity. RUSH your SDI INTRODUCTORY FRANCHISE PACKAGE (including video) to me at once. I'm ordering with the understanding that I have 30 DAYS to review the FRANCHISE OFFER RISK FREE and with no further obligation. If not interested, I may return the FRANCHISE PACKAGE within 30 DAYS for a full refund.
IMPORTANT: SPECIFY □ VHS OR □ BETA (video format)

Enclosed is $50.00 in the form of:
□ I've included $5 extra (total $55) for RUSH FIRST CLASS SHIPPING & HANDLING.
□ Money Order  □ Check  □ VISA  □ MasterCard  □ AMEX  □ Cash

My credit card # _____

Expiration Date: _____  Signature _____

Ship to

Success Dynamics pays postage & handling.  Personal checks delay order 3 weeks.
OFFER VALID ONLY IN THE U.S.
CREDIT CARDS ORDER TOLL FREE: 1-800-223-9026

---------------- DETACH HERE ----------------

### 30 DAY GUARANTEE

Review the SDI FRANCHISE OFFER. If not interested return within 30 days for refund. Full cost of FRANCHISE INTRO PACKAGE IS APPLIED TO FRANCHISE COST WHEN FRANCHISE IS PURCHASED WITHIN 30 DAYS OF RECEIPT OF INTRO PACKAGE. APPLIC- ANTS FAILING TO SECURE A FRANCHISE MAY RECEIVE A FULL REFUND WHEN INTRO PACK IS RETURNED WITHIN 30 DAYS OF NOTIFICATION.

Success Dynamics Inc.
16 State St.
Montpelier, Vermont  05602

DETACH ALONG DOTTED LINE

-------------------- DETACH HERE --------------------

## SUCCESS DYNAMICS, INC.

16 State street
P.O. Box 1087
Montpelier, VT 05602

**YES** I wish to evaluate your SDI franchise opportunity. RUSH your SDI INTRODUCTORY FRANCHISE PACKAGE (including video) to me at once. I'm ordering with the understanding that I have 30 DAYS to review the FRANCHISE OFFER RISK FREE and with no further obligation. If not interested, I may return the FRANCHISE PACKAGE within 30 DAYS for a full refund.
IMPORTANT: SPECIFY ☐ VHS OR ☐ BETA (video format)

Enclosed is $50.00 in the form of:
☐ I've included $5 extra (total $55) for RUSH FIRST CLASS SHIPPING & HANDLING.
☐ Money Order ☐ Check ☐ VISA ☐ MasterCard ☐ AMEX ☐ Cash

My credit card # _____

Expiration Date: _____ Signature _____

Ship to

Success Dynamics pays postage & handling   Personal checks delay order 3 weeks.
OFFER VALID ONLY IN THE U.S.
CREDIT CARDS ORDER TOLL FREE: 1-800-223-9026

DETACH ALONG DOTTED LINE

-------------------- DETACH HERE --------------------

# SUCCESS DYNAMICS, INC.

16 State street
P.O. Box 1087
Montpelier, VT 05602

**YES** I wish to evaluate your SDI franchise opportunity.  RUSH your SDI INTRODUCTORY FRANCHISE PACKAGE (including video) to me at once. I'm ordering with the understanding that I have 30 DAYS to review the FRANCHISE OFFER RISK FREE and with no further obligation. If not interested, I may return the FRANCHISE PACKAGE within 30 DAYS for a full refund.
IMPORTANT: SPECIFY  ☐ VHS OR  ☐ BETA (video format)

Enclosed is $50.00 in the form of:
☐ I've included $5 extra (total $55) for RUSH FIRST CLASS SHIPPING & HANDLING.
☐ Money Order  ☐ Check  ☐ VISA  ☐ MasterCard  ☐ AMEX  ☐ Cash

My credit card # _____

Expiration Date: _____  Signature _____

Ship to

Success Dynamics pays postage & handling.  Personal checks delay order 3 weeks.
OFFER VALID ONLY IN THE U.S.
CREDIT CARDS ORDER TOLL FREE:  1-800-223-9026

DETACH ALONG DOTTED LINE

# SUCCESS DYNAMICS, INC.

16 State street
P.O. Box 1087
Montpelier, VT 05602

**YES** I wish to evaluate your SDI franchise opportunity. RUSH your SDI INTRODUCTORY FRANCHISE PACKAGE (including video) to me at once. I'm ordering with the understanding that I have 30 DAYS to review the FRANCHISE OFFER RISK FREE and with no further obligation. If not interested, I may return the FRANCHISE PACKAGE within 30 DAYS for a full refund.
IMPORTANT: SPECIFY ☐ VHS OR ☐ BETA (video format)

Enclosed is $50.00 in the form of:
☐ I've included $5 extra (total $55) for RUSH FIRST CLASS SHIPPING & HANDLING.
☐ Money Order   ☐ Check   ☐ VISA   ☐ MasterCard   ☐ AMEX   ☐ Cash

My credit card # _____

Expiration Date: _____   Signature _____

Ship to

Success Dynamics pays postage & handling. Personal checks delay order 3 weeks.
OFFER VALID ONLY IN THE U.S.
CREDIT CARDS ORDER TOLL FREE: 1-800-223-9026

---- DETACH HERE ----

## 30 DAY GUARANTEE

Review the SDI FRANCHISE OFFER. If not interested return within 30 days for refund. Full cost of FRANCHISE INTRO PACKAGE IS APPLIED TO FRANCHISE COST WHEN FRANCHISE IS PURCHASED WITHIN 30 DAYS OF RECEIPT OF INTRO PACKAGE. APPLICANTS FAILING TO SECURE A FRANCHISE MAY RECEIVE A FULL REFUND WHEN INTRO PACK IS RETURNED WITHIN 30 DAYS OF NOTIFICATION.

Success Dynamics Inc.
16 State St.
Montpelier, Vermont 05602